# Tales of the Oregon Cascades

by

## Prince Helfrich

Interior Illustrations by
Rod A. MacPherson

**Natural World Press**
Hillsborough, California
1990

ISBN 0-939560-02-X

Library of Congress Cataloging in Publication Data
Helfrich, Prince: 1907—1971
Tales of the Oregon Cascades / by Prince Helfrich
p. cm.
"These essays first appeared in the Register Guard of Eugene, Oregon"—Acknowledgments
1. Natural history—Cascade Range. 2. Natural history—Oregon
I. Title.
QH104.5C3H44 1989
508.795—dc20                                        89—37932
CIP

ATTENTION CONSERVATION ORGANIZATIONS, HIS-
TORICAL SOCIETIES, NORTHWEST BUSINESSES: Quantity discounts are available on bulk purchases of this book for promotions, educational purposes, premiums, or fund-raising. Special books or book excerpts can also be created to fit specific needs. For information, please contact Natural World Press, 607 Chiltern Road, Hillsborough, CA 94010.

# TABLE OF CONTENTS

# Acknowledgments

The publication of these essays would have been impossible without the loving support of my children. They are:

Dave Helfrich and Richard Helfrich, of the Mackenzie River area, whitewater boatmen and guides;

Diane Helfrich Kaldall, of Corvalis, Oregon, reading teacher;

Dean Helfrich, of Springfield, Oregon, riverman and guide.

I am also indebted to Russ and Blyth Carpenter, publishers of Natural World Press, for their special interest in this book.

These essays first appeared in the Register Guard of Eugene, Oregon and are published with their permission.

*Marjorie Peyton Helfrich*

# PRINCE HELFRICH

*From Marjorie Payton Helfrich*

A few men are born to leave their mark in the world. Such a man was Prince Helfrich, riverman, guide and conservationist. Born in 1907 to Eastern Oregon ranching parents, Prince grew up in the era of uncut, old growth trees, and clear sparkling streams.

The family home on the McKenzie River, where his family settled in 1914, was an area of plentiful game and good fishing. Prince was always at home in the woods and nature was his friend.

He told the story of a small boy tracking a grouse for many days by the sound of its drumming call. When the boy finally found the grouse in its secret place, parading and calling on a fallen log, he soon had him in his gun sights. He watched the strutting, proud bird in all his wild beauty. He thought he heard its mate return the call. For long minutes he watched. Finally, he could not reduce this vision to a mass of bloody feathers. He put his gun down and sneaked quietly away to find other game for his mother's dinner table.

Prince attended the University of Oregon and married his college sweetheart. In the ensuing years he taught his three sons and daughter the outdoor skills of boating and fishing, camping and hunting. They learned to appreciate the beauty of wild flowers and native birds. At bedtime, he told them fascinating stories of Indians and animals and early days of pioneers.

Prince loved the challenge of white water rivers. He was the first to run many of the untamed rivers in the Pacific Northwest. He enjoyed people and was among the first guides to take guests safely and comfortably on these wild rivers. He was an accomplished outdoor cook and could produce tasty rainbow trout and Dutch oven biscuits for the enjoyment of his guests.

Prince organized and ran the Skyline Boys Camp, an outdoor fishing camp, for more than 15 years. Young men of twelve to fourteen, who knew only city ways, learned the skills necessary to their comfort and survival in the wilderness. Lessons in fishing and camping and tall tales around the campfire made these trips memorable.

Over the years, as he watched the cutting of the forests, construction of unnecessary roads bisecting the wilderness and damming and polluting of the streams, Prince became a voice for conservation.

In the early 1960's, Prince was asked to write a series of articles for a local newspaper. The pieces in this book are a selection of these articles.

Prince Helfrich died in 1971. He had enriched the lives and experiences of a great many people. His legend will not soon be forgotten.

*From Edward E. Merges*
*Attorney at Law*
*Seattle*

It was late in the 20's at Spark's Ranch on the McKenzie River. An associate of my Dad's had come up from Portland to go fishing and invited me to come along. I was never one to allow my studies at the University to interfere with fishing, so I gathered up my outfit, and we drove up the McKenzie in his old Packard. The folks at Spark's Ranch were helpful and friendly and recommended Prince Helfrich to take us down the river. That he did, and our long friendship began that way.

Prince knew every rock and riffle in the river and could handle the boat and cast a fly like no one else I have ever known. The river and woods, and all the animals and birds, were his life and he lived it to the full. Prince always had the answer and right move in tight situations. And we did have some adventures, I can tell you.

But, probably the most unusual thing about Prince was his personality and ability to help others appreciate the outdoors. His family and friends learned much from him. He made their lives better and more interesting.

Our nights around the campfire are vivid in my memory. Prince's harmonica, mingling with the sounds of night in the forest, often live again in my thoughts. Prince played anything and everything by ear, but mostly those older pieces which brought back memories of a world that has faded away. I like to think that there will always be another time when I will return to camp, perhaps chilled and certainly hungry, and Prince will pull out a piece of jerky for an appetizer while he prepares the campfire biscuits in the iron pot.

The readers will find more in life and the things around them after reading what Prince has written. He was well named indeed.

*From Walter A. Haas, Jr.*
*Honorary Chairman of the Board*
*Levi Strauss & Co.*

Prince and I first met when I was a youngster and he was guiding for Thompson's Lodge on the McKenzie River. Since then, I have been guided by three generations of Helfriches, all extremely competent. Prince taught me most of what I know about fishing and instilled in me a love of the simplicity and beauty of the outdoor life.

He was way ahead of his time as an environmentalist and conservationist, recognized nationally by being asked to testify before Congress on related matters years ago.

As he researched new rivers throughout the Northwest, he usually asked Evie and me on his first guided fishing trip into the latest discovery. We had great times fishing and camping together on the McKenzie, the Klamath, the Rogue, the Deschutes, the Middle Fork, the Blackwater and many other rivers.

He saw the great possibility of Zane Grey's property on the Rogue River. I would never have considered acquiring and developing it without his encouragement and counsel. It has been a great joy to me and my family for 25 years.

Two of the greatest compliments I have ever received were when he invited me to join him, Dave, and Dick on a "family" floating trip down the Rogue River one November. He subsequently asked Evie and me and our daughter, Betsy, to join him and Marjorie on a similar vacation in Montana one summer.

A wonderful man and a treasured friend.

*From Robert W. Straub*
*Former Governor of Oregon*

Oregon rivers were just rivers until we met Prince Helfrich. Running rivers with Prince made them come alive. It was a sublime experience with nature and with outdoor adventure.

Prince had the most sensitive appreciation of nature and of the environment of anyone I have known. Camping out with Prince, I noticed birds would come closer to his campfire with their songs, and deer were more visible and calm. Nature knew a kindred soul in Prince.

My wife Pat and I floated most of Oregon's wild rivers with Prince. He loved the outdoors so much that ali his life he was a student learning more about our precious environment and a teacher making others more aware.

Prince gave Pat and me a most precious gift—a greater sense of awe about nature.

# CHAPTER I

# THE COUNTRY

*Great things are done when men and mountains meet;*
*This is not done by jostling in the street.*

*(William Blake, 1757-1827)*

# MCKENZIE RIVER HISTORY

The first white man to set eyes on the McKenzie River was one of the early-day trappers. In their search for beavers, the mountain men and Hudson Bay trappers covered most all of the main streams. One of the Hudson Bay men, by the name of McKenzie, was traveling up the Willamette River in 1811 and discovered a river coming in from the east. He promptly gave the river his own name. calling it the McKenzie Fork of the Willamette.

Picture the river as it must have been in those days: a clear, cold river untouched by man and teeming with trout and salmon. Birds and game were plentiful. Many deer and elk browsed along the shores, and an occasional Indian trod the paths which closely followed the river.

Some of the old-timers recall the river in the late eighteen hundreds and tell fabulous tales of its fishing. And it is interesting to note that, when the fish were so abundant, they were of small size. The largest trout would average 14 inches. This condition existed because there was not enough food to produce large fish.

In the early days the old-timers tell of driving out from Eugene, with their wagons and teams, and fishing the lower river for two or three days, or until they had a wagon load of fish to take back into town and sell.

As the fish population was diminished, larger fish were

found, and at one time fish (rainbows) of three or four and up
to six pounds were common. Then, with additional fishing
pressure, the great numbers of fish started to decline, so that in
the early 1940's the fish population was in an alarming state.
This is the time that the citizens demanded that something had
to be done and asked the State to look into the situation. A fish
biologist was assigned to the river and increased stocking was
instituted.

First, restocking was done with fingerlings of one to two
inches. These small fry disappeared, and no one knew what
would happen to them. Some probably did not survive and
others fell prey to predators such as kingfishers or larger fish.
The fish population continued to drop. Later on, certain studies
found that the most productive restocking was obtained by
planting legal-sized fish.

Today the program is highly successful, and a sufficient
number of fish are planted to insure reasonable fishing success.
Probably as many fish are planted as are taken out of the river
each year, and the larger native fish left in the stream con-
tribute to the build-up.

I remember when the limit was 60 fish per person. Then it
was reduced to 30, then 20, 15, 10 to the present limit of 5.

The depletion of the stream has been a gradual thing.
Increased fishing, dams, power projects and siltation have all
contributed to the decline.

Only a few of the old timers remember much about the
early McKenzie boating. As you see a light plywood boat float
down the river so safely today, you would not know that at one
time the boats were made of heavy planks, and to take one
down the turbulent rapids was quite a feat.

It was probably in the early 1900's when the first McKenzie
boat was made. Before that, log rafts were used, and perhaps an
Indian canoe slipped down through some of the quieter
stretches. The first boat was a crude affair, made from heavy fir

planks with the cracks caulked with pitch. The planks lapped each other on the sides. The bottom was of wider planks an inch thick. The spaces between were caulked with cotton string and smeared with tar or pitch.

The early boats were 18 feet long and three feet wide in the middle. The sides were from 12 to 15 inches high with a great deal of flare. The seats were just a plank thrown across the gunwales, and under the back seat was a built-in box for the fish.

The boats were heavy, necessitating four men or a team to pull them from the river and load them. The first trailers were not light rubber-tired rigs, but wagons with flatbeds.

After the boat was loaded, the driver and team would take the boat up river a few miles for the next day's fishing trip. Sometimes the fisherman would ride up behind the horse drawn rig with their feet hanging over the edge, with plenty of time to contemplate the scenery and savor the coming fishing trip.

A trip of four or five miles was enough to fairly load the boat with fish. In many places the guide would have to jump out on a riffle and hold the boat while his passengers fished. When Martin Rapids was reached, the boat was lined around. It was not until about 1924 that daring guides started running the rapids, and then it was without passengers.

In those days it was necessary to carry a big water bucket for bailing after running the rapids. It was nothing to fill the boat to the floor boards in such places as Clover Point, Martin, McAllister, and Gate Creek Rapids. And if a guide came in at the end of the day not soaking wet to the waist, he had not put in much of a day.

With boating on the McKenzie at least 80 years old, the present-day boat is a far cry from the first boats used. Our plywood boats are wide with high sides, but lightweight, and shaped to run the rough water. The five-ply bottom of half-inch plywood is tough and waterproof. Today's boatman drifts down the river with little effort and keeps a dry boat all day long. There are some of the old days we would not care to go back to.

# UNUSUAL MOUNTAIN NAMES

As you look over a U.S. Forest Service map, you will notice many unusual names. Some places keep their original Indian names, while others refer to people or incidents. "Scott" occurs many times on the map. This was the name of an early-day leader who guided the first party of white men up the McKenzie Valley and over the Cascades. Separation Creek is thusly called because it separates The Husband from The Wife.

When the first land surveys were being made in the McKenzie country, a group of surveyors were camped in the high mountains south of Blue River. Their food supply was running low, but the job was almost finished so they decided to stick it out. Towards the last, they ran completely out of baking powder and had to make bread without any leavening. The resulting biscuits were so hard and indigestible that someone called them "death balls." A mountain in that vicinity still bears that name.

Back in about 1904, a party of hunters with horses and pack burros were making their way down the South Fork. The party was following an old indian trail part of the time and making their own trail the rest. This was before a Forest Service trail had been built up the South Fork.

At one bad place the trail switched back high above the river. When the burros came to this spot, one of them crowded the other over the bank. This one was the most valued pack animal on the trip, as he carried the Dutch oven and a gallon of jug whiskey.

Rolling end over end, the luckless animal fell some 150 feet to the rocks below. The fall killed the burro and broke the cast iron Dutch oven, but the jug of whiskey was still intact.

The broken Dutch oven was later hung in a tree nearby, and since then the spot has always been known as Dutch Oven Camp.

# AT STEENS MOUNTAINS

In the dim geological past a tremendous event occurred in Southeastern Oregon. Suddenly, or perhaps over a period of years, a great block of the earth's surface was upthrust.

Tipping to the west and presenting a great wall to the east, the fault block rose some 5,000 feet. The western slope was gradual and allowed streams to form and cut deep canyons, while the eastern slope remained almost a vertical wall. Today this area stands as a unique formation and an escarpment of interest to all who visit its rugged grandeur.

It is truly a wild and impressive scene from the top of the Steens Mountains. From the summit of this steep escarpment the immense Alvord Desert, the mountains in Idaho to the east, and the high Nevada mountains to the south can be seen.

The canyons of the Blitzen and Kiger gorges, which open before you to the west, drop 2,000 to 3,000 feet to the floor of the valley below. Rugged ledges of rock offer fine places of concealment for deer and mountain lynx. In the U-shaped valley the small clear Blitzen winds its way, the banks of the stream lined with willow and cottonwood. In the fall, the clumps of golden aspen glow brightly against the gray rocky bluffs.

In the high desert country of the Steens are found many flowers and plants, some of which have never been identified. Although it is a complete desert flora, one isolated canyon contains a fine growth of white firs. The balance of larger trees and shrubs are mountain mahogany and quaking aspen.

Typical desert fauna consisting of jack rabbits, coyotes, antelope, sage grouse and lynx cats are still found in abundance. Mule deer inhabit all of the area, and of late the State has liberated a number of big horn sheep. Many years ago sheep were found here, but the last of the original band disappeared in the early part of the century. It is hoped that they will become numerous again.

The tremendous gorges of the western slope have been cut by small streams snow fed from the high peaks. The top of the Steens is more than 9,000 feet in elevation. Snow may fall as early as September, and hunting parties have been snowbound for several days in October. Several smaller canyons open into the main Blitzen Gorge; Big and Little Indian Creeks and Fish Creek contain nice rainbows and empty into the Blitzen River, where they are finally lost in Malheur Lake.

# SKI TRIP TO CLEAR LAKE

Wilderness has given way to a modern highway, but at one time the upper McKenzie and Clear Lake were completely inaccessible except by a dim trail.

The trail led up the valley from Belknap Springs. It crossed the McKenzie at Smith River at about the site of the present Carmen-Smith dam, then began to climb up a long ridge between Kink Creek and the river, eventually crossing the lava fields near Koosah and Sahalie Falls and again crossing the McKenzie on a fallen tree near the outlet of Clear Lake.

An old trapper's cabin stood on the shore of the lake whose crystal depths still reveal submerged trees. Beavers had probably been taken from the lake in the early 1900's. A modern campground now occupies the spot.

In midwinter of 1928, a companion and I left Belknap Springs with small packs on our backs and headed for a weekend of skiing at Clear Lake. A light dusting of snow was on the ground where we first hit the trail, and, as we gained elevation, the snow rapidly increased in depth. By the time we reached Smith River, it was necessary to put on skis.

Darkness was just beginning to fall as we crossed the old log bridge on the McKenzie, and we started looking for a place to camp. No snags with good bark or pitch stumps were found, so we continued until we were well up on the ridge and getting out of the deep shadows of the valley. The moon was coming out with a little light filtering down through the tall trees.

Deceptive shadows fell across the quiet snowy trail.

We stopped and brewed a tin can of tea and decided to continue. A few blazes were visible, and the snow was getting deeper. More experienced men would have stopped and found a good camp, but in the exuberance of youth and the excitement of a moonlight wilderness, we pushed on.

Soon we came to the long lava flows jutting down like stone fingers on the slopes from Belknap Crater. In the open country it was like daylight. By this time we had lost the trail, which was now covered with six feet of crusted snow. But we could hear the noise of the river and thought we were going in the right direction.

After traveling for an hour or two, we realized the wind had changed and we could distinctly hear the roar of the falls. We knew they were fairly near the outlet of the lake. But now the sound came from far down the canyon, so we knew we had passed the falls and must turn and retrace our steps in order to find the outlet of the lake and the crossing log.

We were both getting tired but kept going in order to find a good camp in the timber. The complete lack of shadows on the bright snow made it impossible to see little depressions, and we would frequently fall heavily with our packs on our backs and our skis on.

At last we reached the outlet of the lake and noted that the lower end was frozen over. The ice looked unsafe, so we decided to make camp there and hunt the footlog in the morning. Knowing that there was a cabin on the lake, my friend let out a tremendous yell. If someone was at that cabin, they would probably call back and direct us there.

As the echoes of his voice died away, we thought we heard an answer from the upper end of the lake. Calling again we heard the answer, and this time we identified the long drawn-out howl of a timber wolf. With timber wolves howling around us, and only one small hand ax, we were spurred to get a fire going as rapidly as possible.

While we cut down a green hemlock and cut it in short lengths to make a base in the snow for our fire, the wolves answered one another from one ridge to the next. To say that the hair was standing up on the backs of our necks is not stretching the truth, as there is no more blood-curdling sound in all the wilderness.

After getting a good fire going with pitch and dry bark, we cut boughs and placed them on the snow near the fire and curled up in a blanket each.

We slept fitfully until a cold rain began about daylight. Then we ate a small snack of jerky and started out to find the log across the McKenzie. Crossing this log when it was covered with several feet of snow presented quite a formidable job, but soon we were on the trail that led to the cabin.

The old cabin was a welcome sight. While my companion built a fire in the stove, I made a pan of biscuits. These disappeared in a hurry, and we prepared to catch up on sleep.

On the sagging bed was an old mattress and several ragged quilts, but we covered up with them and were soon asleep. In late afternoon we awoke to a decidedly unpleasant odor. We had slept in a nest of dead mice.

Again we cooked up a big feed of stew and hot bread and then set out to explore the surrounding country before it got dark. My friend put on his skis and started down the slope to the lake. This was a faster run than we anticipated, and my friend ended up by skiing right out into the lake waist deep. However, this didn't stop our exploration and, after looking over the big springs at the upper end of the lake, we returned to the cabin for the night.

Next day we skied up to Fish Lake and noted many wolf tracks along the creek bottom. No deer were wintering in this high area, but we saw many rabbit tracks. These we hoped would be the wolves' regular diet.

After another night at the cabin, we started back home in a thick snow storm. Pausing at the brink of the falls, we stopped to take a picture of this beautiful sight in its winter garb. The snow was again obliterating the trail, and we had to make our way along by guess. We felt lost in this great white world of whirling flakes. By listening carefully, the roar of the river could occasionally be heard, and this determined our route down the valley. It was getting dark before we reached Smith River Ridge.

The woods were muffled and silent as the snow continued to fall. My friend was ahead, and, as he crossed the bridge, he noted a big wolf track going in the same direction that we were heading. It was smoking fresh and not yet filled with snow. A few minutes later, as I approached the bridge, I saw a second wolf disappearing in the gathering darkness. Apparently we were all trying to cross the bridge at the same time.

After another two hours on the trail, with the help of a dim flashlight and pitch torches, we arrived back into Belknap Springs. The sights and experiences we had enjoyed will not be duplicated by many modern men, because the howl of the timber wolf is almost a thing of the past.

✦

# THREE SISTERS

Smoke was rising from a hundred campfires. Small groups of people were gathered around the arrowhead makers, while others were hunting the open meadows intent on picking up pieces of obsidian suitable for working into arrowheads and knives.

The time was a century ago, and this was an Indian encampment gathered here on their annual trip to the great volcanic glass deposits on the slopes of the Middle Sister.

For only a few months of the year can this high area be used. The rest of the time it is snowbound from the heavy Pacific storms that bathe the western slopes of the Cascades. But the few months that it can be used are ideal for camping and exploring the many valleys and peaks.

Cold, clear streams come down from the glaciers above, and the little meadows abound with many colored flowers of the high alpine country. Here are found the trees so well known to the Cascades, including white-barked pine, mountain hemlock, alpine fir and maple fir.

Here also are the homes of the coneys and whistling marmots—little animals indigenous to this area who spend six months of the year under the snow. In summer, the country is invaded by the migratory animals such as deer, elk and bear, who live here only the few short months of summer.

At daybreak you may hear the call of the Oregon jay telling

the others of his flock he has found food. Soon there will be several, floating into camp on silent wings, begging for a handout. From the top of a tall snag will come the raucous call of a Clark's nutcracker. He is also of the jay family, but a very noisy one.

Obsidian is a product of volcanic action. Occurring with it will be scoria, pumice and volcanic bombs (bubbles of hot lava that have solidified, leaving a hollow center). An interesting feature is that whole areas are literally covered with obsidian fragments. It glistens like acres of broken glass.

From this base camp one can take interesting trips both north and south on the Skyline Trail or climb the nearby Middle Sister. Another interesting trip is west from Obsidian Camp out on an open plateau, bounded on three sides by the high obsidian cliffs.

# MEADOW TO FOREST

A long string of Indian ponies wound down the narrow trail and out into the big meadow. Riders dismounted, packs were thrown off, horses were staked out and preparations were soon made for a night's camp. The time was many years ago, and this was the annual trek of the Warm Springs Indians from Eastern Oregon to the valleys of Western Oregon.

The green meadows were the favorite camping places of the Indians. Here was found an abundance of horse feed, and the hunters could stalk deer and elk more successfully. In the High Cascades, meadows were found everywhere. The carpet of thick grass was dotted here and there by scanty clumps of trees. But unknown to these early dwellers, the great meadows were destined to slowly disappear. For a great many years, the meadows had remained the same because of the fall burning of the dry grass, which discouraged the encroachment of the forest. But with the coming of the white men, conditions were to change.

Soon large flocks of sheep were to pasture in these meadows and, with the cutting of the tough turf by thousands of tiny sharp hoofs, a favorable bed was made for the seeds of the conifers. Now with all burning stopped, the trees gradually began to reach out into the open spaces. Today, many of these meadows have disappeared and others show a steady march of little trees out from the borders.

The only meadows that can remain in their present state will be the wet swampy ones where trees will not grow, or the dry hillsides of scanty soil where a tree cannot get started.

With the disappearance of many meadows, a new problem is beginning to arise. When a bear comes out of hibernation in April or May, his source of food is very limited. Some old winter kills of deer and elk may furnish him with a few meals, but usually he depends on green vegetation that is found in swamps and hillside meadows. With green grass and wild cucumber gone, the next best thing is the inner bark of conifer trees.

To get at the inner cambium layer a bear will take his claws and tear the tough outer bark away, then gnaw the juicy inner bark. The tree may be completely girdled and killed, or it may be only damaged. And here is an interesting feature to a forester. A partly damaged tree will bear a heavier cone crop than a fast growing one. Thus, nature works to offset the damage done by bears by producing an abundance of seeds.

# INDIAN MIGRATIONS

As a boy living in the McKenzie Valley in the early 1900's, I remember the coming of the Indians each summer. They came to catch and dry salmon and to pick huckleberries in the high mountains before their return to Eastern Oregon, where they wintered in the Warm Springs Valley of the Deschutes. Before the white men settled the Willamette Valley, the Indians had used the old trails over the Cascades, but by the turn of the century they were using the white man's roads.

Horses were still employed for transportation and the column would appear down the road in a long string with all the dogs following. Although some of the Indians drove wagons, the majority of the members rode ponies. Small children, too little to mount their horses, would climb up to the saddle on a long string attached to the saddle horn. Extremely old Indians would dismount by sliding down a string.

I recall an old Indian who slid off his horse this way and stretched out on a blanket. On inquiring if the old man was sick, I was told the he was an old, old man—107 summers old.

That night I talked to the old man through an interpreter. He told me many tales of his younger days—of his annual coming to the McKenzie Valley over the old Indian trails through the Cascades, of his hunts and the killing of bear, deer and elk, and the burning of the brush in the fall to make more hunting ground. He told in detail of the great game trails where they would lie in wait for the deer and elk, and how the Indians would drive the game through a runway to other Indians, who were waiting with bows and arrows.

Brush would be burned in the fall as the Indians returned to Eastern Oregon. Since it was late in the season, the fall rains would soon extinguish the fires, before any great damage was done. The burning made easier access through the country, as well as foraging for horses and big game animals.

Little flats and open meadows along the river afforded them good camping grounds, and, around these old camping grounds, one can still find an occasional arrow point or broken skinning knife. They were made from obsidian, found in the numerous volcanic deposits near the base of the Three Sisters. At Obsidian Camp on the Skyline Trail, the ground is still covered with broken fragments of volcanic glass, and many of the pieces of obsidian show that they have been worked by the early-day red man.

These seasonal treks to the western valley were duplicated both north and south of the Three Sisters area. The Willamette and Santiam rivers were widely used for hunting and fishing, and the old trails led back through the Cascades to the Indians' wintering grounds.

# CASCADE INDIAN CAMPS

High in the Cascades, around huckleberry patches, near large meadows, or on the shores of glacial lakes, one can still find remnants of old Indian camps. A piece of obsidian, a broken pestle, a depression in the rocks where seeds were ground or an Indian rock sign may be the clue.

The Indian tribes of Central Oregon would come into the Cascades each summer to camp, hunt, fish, and gather the luscious blue huckleberries of the high country. The old trails led through several different passes from Eastern Oregon and down the western slopes to the valleys of the Willamette River.

Today one can still find the deeply trenched trails or old artifacts left around the camps. One of the more accessible camps is on the north end of Indian Ridge. Here is still visible the rock signs which probably marked the entrance to a camp or the presence of a good huckleberry patch. Deep paths lead across a bare grass ridge or down a hill into a meadow where numerous fragments of arrowheads or skinning knives indicate this was a favorite camping place.

Picture an Indian camp a century ago, with the tepees scattered around in sheltered spots, the squaws gathering and drying berries, the braves out hunting, the horses picketed out to graze and the old men gathered around little fires working on arrow points or skinning knives. A supply of obsidian or other hard rock was always at hand for the never-ending job of making tools.

As you wander around an old camp looking for arrowheads or dig deep in the ashes of an old fire pit, you are taken back a hundred years or more when this country was still unexplored and untouched by the hand of the white man.

# HUCKLEBERRY SEASON

September has always been the month when the Indians would gather their winter's supply of huckleberries. With the coming of early fall, they would go into the high mountains, camp at the berry patch and pick and dry large quantities of the luscious blueberries.

Only a few localities had good berries. They grew at an elevation of 5,000 feet.　The country must be open to grow the small bushes. Gold Hill and the Tibbits was a favorite patch, as was Indian Ridge and Packsaddle Mountain farther south, and Mount Hood in the north.

Picture an Indian encampment on one of the high ridges in the Cascades, with the younger people bringing armloads of broken branches laden with the fruit to the old squaws, who would beat them off the bushes, dropping them on blankets. Later the berries would be rolled down other sloping blankets to clean them of sticks and leaves, then sun-dried and stored in buckskin bags.

In the early days, the Indians would winter in Central Oregon where the climate was dry, then, with the coming of early summer, they would cross the Cascades on old established trails to hunt and fish in the lush valleys of the western side. Some of their old hunting trails are still visible on the ridges of the higher mountains. With the passing of hundreds of horses over a trail, the path would be cut down to almost a trench. At certain places, rock signs would be placed to indicate a camp, a water hole or deer crossing.

As the summer progressed and the Chinook salmon came into the rivers to spawn, the Indians would move down in the valleys to spear and trap the big fish. Long wooden racks would be built to dry them on, with a slow fire burning underneath to keep the flies away. Prepared this way, the fish would keep through the winter.

Even as late as 1925, I can remember the Indians coming every fall. They had horses and wagons then, but still made the trip for salmon and berries.

The white families living on the river would save their deer hides to trade with the Indians. One deer hide for a pair of moccasins or two pairs of gloves would be the usual bargain. Sometimes the moccasins would have to be made and brought back the following year. In the case of the children, a careful measurement would be taken, and proper allowances made for fast-growing feet. The Indians never failed to deliver the moccasins the next year.

I'll never forget one old Indian who had his foot all wrapped in a gunny sack and was limping badly. When my mother asked him what was the matter with his foot, he grunted "step on em-horse."

With the coming of fine highways and fast automobiles, the only thing that can remind one of the old Indian trails and encampments is the occasional opportunity to find an arrow head or piece of sharp obsidian used by the passing red man.

# INDIANS VALUED OBSIDIAN

Ribbons of smoke rose from the fires around the Indian encampment. Here and there small groups were gathered around the fires cooking, eating or talking, but at least one of the campers was engaged in the never-ending job of making arrowheads or knives. He was the artist, chipping away at bits of rock or bone, making the tools for hunters and craftsmen.

A careful scrutiny of any old Indian campground will turn up small chips of black, shiny rock. This is obsidian, the volcanic glass material from which arrow points, skinning knives and other tools were made.

Only a few places in Oregon produce obsidian. One of these is up on the high ridges of the Middle Sister. Here, on the Skyline Trail, you can walk across glittering paved fields of it. Another is Glass Butte in Central Oregon. Indians came for hundreds of miles to secure this rock, and it was so valuable to their way of living that it was sometimes used in trade for goods. Taking a supply along on their travels, they would sit around the fire fashioning their future weapons. Heads for arrows and sharp cutting knives were the most important uses; they would also make awls, punches, diggers, scrapers and hammers from this hard black rock.

Making tools and arrowheads was a great art in the early-day culture of the Indians. Some tribes did beautiful work as shown by the collections from their area, while other tribes made only crude tools for utilitarian uses. Today a few white men have mastered the art of making arrowheads and turn out work as well done as any old Indian craftsmen. The tools used in making an arrow point are a heavy protective glove or hide for the hand holding the rock, and the sharp, tough point of a deer's horn.

Chipping is done by pressure with the tip of the horn. Little flakes are broken off, with the rock soon taking the desired shape. I have seen a good craftsmen make an arrowhead from the thick glass of a broken coke bottle.

A few arrowheads are found around the edges of dried up lakes. In shooting at water fowl, the hunters would lose their arrows. On the hunting grounds, arrows would be lost when shot at game. But the lucky artifact hunter is the one who finds a cache of arrowheads in some cave or buried around an old encampment. Many fine specimens have been found in caves or laying on the ground of some ancient camp, where wind or water has uncovered them.

# INDIAN ARTIFACTS

Not long ago, a cowboy was searching for horses in the Catlow Valley of Southeastern Oregon near the Steens Mountain. A sudden snow storm blew up, and he sought shelter at the base of some high cliffs. While looking around for something with which to build a fire, he noted an opening leading back into a cave. He investigated and found a good-sized room back in the rocks, whose roof was black from fires of many years ago. Lying on the sandy floor of the cave was an obsidian skinning knife.

This is one of the finest discoveries of ancient Indian habitation that has been made for many years. The cowboy said that he had ridden by those cliffs a thousand times and had never before noted any opening at their base. Subsequent to this discovery, several more caves have been found in that vicinity, all showing signs of fire.

Among the things found in the first cave were a pair of sagebrush sandals, complete with fiber tying strings, a large mat made from reeds, part of a basket, and numerous pieces of obsidian tools.

A look at the geology of the country shows that the caves were once on the shores of an ancient lake, long since dried up. Only sagebrush grows on what was once the bed of the lake. The entire Steens Mountain area has been a favorite place to hunt arrowheads. Little vegetation covers the ground and the wind constantly uncovers new finds. Dry Lake, on the east side of the Steens, has been famous for its arrowheads and spear points.

This must have been wonderful ground for the Indians in the early days. The mountains and desert held many different kinds of animals, and the surrounding lakes were teeming with fish. Arrowheads found on the shores of the ancient lakes are evidence of the abundance of ducks and geese once found there.

When hunting Indian artifacts, keep in mind such places as camp grounds near springs or lakes, animal runways and wild fowl habitat.

# TRAILS ARE STILL THERE

Dust was rising from a long string of horses winding along a narrow pass between the Middle and South Sister. It was spring in the High Cascades, and an occasional snow bank blocked their way. In the valleys of the western slope, it was already summer.

This was the annual trek of the Indians from the wintering grounds in Eastern Oregon to the lush green valleys of the McKenzie. Here they would fish and hunt all summer, drying great quantities of salmon, deer and elk for the coming winter. On the trip back to the Warm Springs on the Deschutes, they would stop long enough to gather and dry the luscious wild huckleberries found only in the high mountains.

On many of the high ridges in the Cascades, one still sees remnants of the old Indian trails. They are cut deep in the open grass-covered ridges by the annual passing of hundreds of Indian ponies. The ridges were their best access to the lower country; in a few instances, the old Indian trails followed the stream valleys.

One such trail followed the McKenzie from Clear Lake downstream. Where huge windfalls were encountered, the Indians would build a ramp leading up one side and down the other. Thus, through the passing of thousands of hooves, the log would be gradually worn down. The trail led past the present Belknap Hot Springs, where the red men would camp, sometimes leaving ailing members to bathe in the hot water.

Some of the ridges where the old trails are still visible are Lowder Mountain, Olallie Trail, Hiyu and Indian Ridge. Many camps, now identified by the finding of obsidian artifacts, were located along these routes.

The top of Lowder Mountain must have been a favorite camp, judging from the remnants of old fires. The flat-topped mountain might have been a ceremonial ground, as it commanded a view in all directions. Two ice-cold springs added to the convenience. Indian Holes and Squaw Holes must have been their favorite hunting camps. They had water, an abundance of grass, and were in the heart of the summer range for deer and elk.

Many of our present names have stemmed from Indian usage—Hiyu Ridge, Kotsuck Butte, Olallie Trail, Tenas Lakes, Tipso Mountain and Calapooya River.

As fall approached, before the early snows in the high mountains, the Indians would start back to their wintering grounds in the Warm Springs Valley.

# HIKE INTO WILDERNESS

We shouldered our packs in late afternoon on the start of a week's trip into the wilderness country.

The deep, dark canyon was almost a rain forest, with heavy moss carpeting the ground and dense stands of old-growth fir, cedar and hemlock.

It was a country of much moisture with little creeks coming down all the steep-sided canyons, and clear, cold springs emerging from the overhanging banks along the trail. Maidenhair fern lined the banks in precise, symmetrical rows of delicate green. Various shrubs, including salmonberry and thimbleberry, were in late bloom. It was still spring here, although the calendar showed that it was July.

This heavily timbered country does not attract the number of birds that may be found elsewhere. But we did see and hear the varied thrush, the red-breasted robin, the russet-backed thrush, winter wren, water ouzel and kingfisher. In the distance we also heard the drumming of a woodpecker and the lonely call of the white-breasted nuthatch. A covey of grouse flushed near the trail, the young about half-grown.

We hit a few patches of snow as we climbed to around 3,000 feet. Camp was made in a small grassy valley, where we found good firewood from some old snags.

The next morning we crossed several creeks on wet, slick logs. On one of these we came close to losing our entire sack of cooking equipment. One of the boys lost his balance and dropped the packsack in the swirling stream below, and we had visions of having to cook our fish on sharp sticks for the rest of the trip. The pack was swept away rapidly, but quick action and the lucky position of a log jam saved the day.

In this pack we carried two or three nesting cans, a fry pan, a small reflector oven, grill and aluminum foil. Each member of our party carried his own cup, foil plate, spoon, and pocket knife. In our food sacks we had some biscuits and cornbread mix, as well as puddings and sweets. We were going to rely rather heavily on fish, so while the equipment dried in the sun, we cut poles from willow and began the game of catching mountain cutthroat trout.

One must sneak up to a pool very quietly and drop a fly in with as little disturbance as possible to fool these beautiful, fat little trout. They are marked with black spots, a red slash on the throat, and have fins tipped with scarlet.

In late afternoon of the second day, we surprised a band of elk feeding in a meadow below us. We heard the crash of underbrush as an old cow elk, who was standing guard for the herd, gave the signal for danger. We caught glimpses of tawny hides and dark manes as they left the clearing.

That night we camped at a small mountain lake where we found a pair of mallards nesting. At dusk the deer came out to investigate our camp, and after dark we heard their soft footfalls. The lake lay quietly as darkness descended. Not a ripple stirred the surface, but the distant murmur of a stream designated its outlet. Venus hung in the western sky; soon it would imperceptibly sink into the black horizon. We slept, but tomorrow we would explore another valley.

# WILD BERRY TIME

How many of you have had the pleasure of taking a pail and going into the woods for wild berries? The pail must be just right. It must not be too large and should be one of the old buckets that shortening or lard come in. It must be slung from the waist by a rope or string so that the picker can use both hands.

As you enter the berry patch, the squirrels and birds will try to warn you away. An old mother grouse with her brood will fly away from their territory. Another grouse and her brood will fly away to perch and cluck from a fir tree. A flock of wild pigeons will wing by and alight in an old snag to wait their turn at the berry patch.

The gathering of berries was a special time for the Indians in the early days. The seasons, to them, were times to gather certain foods. In the spring there were fresh greens to pick. Later on salmon came into the rivers, and they must be caught and dried. As roots and seeds matured, they also must be gathered and stored for the winter. Early fall was for picking and drying berries.

The most highly prized berry was the mountain huckleberry, found only in the high open country above 5,000 feet. Here the luscious blue and black berries grew in great profusion from low bushes without stickers or thorns. The Indians would cut the brush with the berries still clinging to the branches and beat the berries onto blankets. The blanket was gently sloping so that the round berries would roll to one end and into a container, but leaves and trash would stick to the blanket.

Great quantities must be gathered and spread out in the sun to dry. After they were thoroughly dried, they were packed into sacks or other containers for the winter. Some were mixed with meat and tallow to form pemmican.

Many of the old huckleberry patches are still available. In some places encroaching trees are crowding them out, but, in open country, around rock slides and bear grass patches, huckleberry patches are still abundant. Mountains such as Gold Hill, Carpenter, Indian Ridge, Packsaddle, Irish, Grasshopper, and Hiyu Ridge have accessible berry patches.

There are several other wild berries that make good jam or jelly. The red huckleberry can be found in wooded areas at lower elevations. Blue elderberries make excellent jelly. And for something different, try Oregon grape for a tart jelly. Blackcaps or wild raspberries are numerous in cutover land, and you should not overlook the wild evergreen blackberry found in most any pasture and along streams.

With an old lard pail over your arm and a lunch tucked in your jacket, forget the busy world and spend a peaceful day in the fields or mountains.

# THE DOUGLAS FIR CYCLE

The first warm east winds of early fall had started to blow. The cones growing on the high limbs of a Douglas fir standing on a ridge were the first to respond. Very slowly they opened to release their precious load.

All summer the tiny seeds had been forming in the cone. Attached to each seed was a little wing that was to play an important part when the seed was finally released.

Each seed was covered by a cup-like scale, and sticking out from under the scale was the three-pronged bract so characteristic of the Douglas Fir. The cone, seared to a rich brown, was beginning to open. A gentle wind would carry the winged seed far out over the forest.

Some would land on logs, a leaf or a moss bed, never to play their part in nature. Some would be eaten by squirrels or mice. A very few would find their way to the soil, and, lying there through the long winter, would eventually sprout and start a tree.

This is the beginning of the Douglas fir. The first year it is no more than two inches tall—a little tassel not unlike the end of a fir branch. The second year it may grow to six inches in height and from here on, a steady growth of from a few inches to several feet is possible.

Under good growing conditions, which means plenty of sunlight, a tall shoot reaches always higher and higher. A whorl of tiny limbs indicates that another year has passed. It is possible to approximate the age of a tree by counting the whorls of limbs.

The first few years of growth are filled with many dangers. A passing deer may nip the growing bud, a rabbit may nibble the succulent tip, a wood rat may cut the tiny tree for its nest, a porcupine may girdle the tree, or a heavy growth of brush may shut the sunshine out. But in 10 to 15 year the spike-like tip is growing towards the sky, and many dangers are left behind.

Now the growth is rapid. An increase of an inch in diameter is possible each year. In 40 or 50 years it may be harvested as a pole or piling. In 80 to 100 years it is a second growth tree ready for small sawlogs. And in another 50 to 60 years it will grow into old growth with the possibility of great smooth logs that can be made into plywood. Some get to be 12 feet or more in diameter.

During the life of a tree there is the ever-present danger of fire, wind and the various fungi and insects. Very few trees reach ripe old age without the scars of some infirmity.

The first sign of over-age in a tree will be a dead top. A tree normally dies from the top down. The top will die, decay and drop out. Later another section may fall. It is then called a snag top and will still have a few green limbs. Growth will continue and the base of the tree will still be sound.

In the end the snag will eventually fall and decay, forming rich soil for another generation. Young trees will spring up all around as sunlight is again reaching the ground. The cycle will begin anew.

# FOREST FRAGRANCES

The quiet of dusk was approaching as we neared camp. Suddenly there came to us the scent of wood smoke, pungent and unmistakable. We knew then that we would soon catch sight of our little tent pitched beside the lake.

Among the delights of wilderness, one can count on the variety of odors and fragrances. These may vary depending on the season of the year and the location. But one who is familiar with the outdoors knows that distinctive odors characterize certain areas, and a puff of smoke or whiff of pine may recall trips or experiences sharply to memory.

There is the delicate, sweet smell of the first spring flowers—white and pink heather, penstemon, shooting star or mountain lily—all found in high alpine meadows. There is the clean, fresh smell of earth after a summer rain. The person who loves the wilderness will recall the spicy fragrance of balsam boughs under the sleeping bag, the sharp odor of cinnamon leaf on a hot hillside, and the dank smell of skunk cabbage growing in a swamp.

One of the most satisfying fragrances of all is that of a deep, dark old-growth forest. One gets a composite of many odors: the smell of evergreens and conifers, the dampness of moss, the scent of mold and leaves, the decaying duff on the forest floor, and the aroma of crushed needles on the trail. It is an odor indescribable, but unique and never forgotten.

When one crosses the divide into Eastern Oregon a whole

new variety of odors are present. There is the scent of pine forests, the tangy scents of sagebrush, and the strong smell of juniper. The air itself has dryness instead of moisture.

Have you ever noticed the fresh, wonderful fragrance of water in a little creek or spring when you have stopped along the trail and bent down to quench your thirst?

Water has an odor, and animals may be drawn from miles away by this smell when they are thirsty. There is a difference, too, in the smell of water when it is in a swift-flowing stream or river where the breaking bubbles of a rapids have a particularly fresh odor, or that of a vast, quiet lake whose surface is scarcely stirred by a breath of air. As a river approaches the sea, one may sometimes catch the salty tang in the air when the sea itself is still 50 miles away.

Animals use their sense of smell much more than that of sight or hearing. They can stand motionless at the edge of a valley or the entrance to a canyon and know all that is going on. They constantly test the wind for the reports it brings to them. The man who spends a great deal of his time in the wilderness also knows that the animals have special odors, and he may sometimes be able to tell that a bear has recently passed that way or that a herd of elk has crossed the trail ahead of him.

Fires, too, have distinctive odors. The smell of the early morning campfire differs from that of the late evening fire, and one who has camped often will never forget the smell of a fire made with huge slabs of pungent fir bark.

It is refreshing to get away from the civilized smells of exhaust pipes, mills, and people, and enjoy the odors of the wilderness.

# WARMING FIRE

This series of articles will explore survival in the outdoors. One of the first things to consider is warmth. A person can go for days without food, but warmth is necessary the first night. And warmth will come from a fire. If we assume you have either matches or a lighter, the first thing to do is find dry wood or other dry fuel. This is obtainable from a dead tree or snags, small dry twigs, fir cones, dry leaves or from the underneath surface of an old log. Of course, the very best fire building material is fir or pine pitch. It is found in a dead tree or snag or even a rotten log, and it will always be dry.

The shave stick method of starting a fire is the one most commonly used. This requires a sharp knife or axe. To make a shave stick, hold any stick or wood firmly with one hand while cutting fine shavings with a knife or axe. The shavings are not cut completely off but cling to the wood, forming a fuzzy bunch of fine wood. Soft woods such as fir, pine or cedar are the best.

When a sufficient pile of shavings has been accumulated, touch a match to the finest and slowly add the other shavings. As a little tongue of flame reaches up through the wood, add other dry pieces until a good blaze is obtained. In starting a fire it is best to place it between two sticks, pieces of bark, or other material to hold it slightly off the ground and allow a draft underneath. In starting a fire under difficult conditions, do not allow too much air space between sticks but pack them quite closely together and all pointing in the same direction.

When a good fire is going, add larger pieces of wood. A fire built of heavy bark will last all night. For maximum warmth, build the fire out several feet from a log, rock or tree and place yourself next to the obstruction. It will act as a reflector.

Almost any kind of wood will burn, but some are better than others. Avoid hemlock or white fir. The soft woods such as alder, maple, ash or vine maple are all good fuel. In fact, a fire can be started from a green tree by shaving it very fine and using the heartwood. It will slowly burn into a hot fire. An experienced woodsman will almost always use a piece of pitch and the outside bark of a fir tree. An axe is a great help, but not a necessity in starting a fire. A pocket knife is a "must" in the woods.

When one has a good fire going, one has the basic necessities of a camp: warmth, protection and food preparation.

# SHELTER MEANS SURVIVAL

When confronted with the necessity of spending a night in the woods, the first requirement is warmth, and we will assume that you can build a fire. The second need is shelter, and the wilderness abounds in shelters you need only to find or make.

A natural shelter would be a cave, an overhanging rock ledge, a big windfall or a tree with thick branches. Primitive man found permanent shelter and protection in caves or shallow openings under rock ledges, but these are not easily found. The next best thing would be a shelter formed by a big windfall several feet above the ground, or even a hollow tree large enough for a bed. A few species of trees offer excellent shelter from a storm. A white fir with thick sloping branches is almost like a tent, and a cedar or fir leaning at an angle will offer a dry spot for a camp.

Besides a shelter to keep out the storm, you need a nook to catch and hold the warmth from a fire. This is obtained from a tree, rock or log at the rear of your camp. The heat strikes the obstruction and is reflected to you.

When a natural shelter is lacking, the second best camp is a lean-to. This is a framework of poles or branches thatched with any available material: green boughs, bark, moss, grass or leaves. A ridge pole can be secured by placing one end in the fork of a tree with the other end on a log or in a second tree. From the ridge pole a framework can be made by using smaller poles or branches.

On this sloping frame the thatching material can be woven to make it completely waterproof. When thatching, start at the bottom and work up layer by layer, so each succeeding layer covers the top of the one underneath. In this way water will run down the outside and not drip through.

Large slabs of fir or cedar bark are the finest thatching material for a waterproof shelter, but a steeply sloping shelter thatched heavily with green boughs will also turn the rain.

# FOOD FROM STREAMS

For a person living in the woods and trying to survive entirely on plant life, the diet would be monotonous and lacking in nutrition. Therefore, some meat should be added. Let us examine the possibilities of getting this food from lakes or streams.

Fishing would be the answer, but not all individuals are fishermen. Some of them would starve even with all the modern tackle, as evidenced by the ordinary angler's luck on our Oregon streams. But with a minimum of tackle and the know-how, a person could catch sufficient fish to live. A short piece of line, a fine leader, and a small hook would be necessary. A pole could be cut from any straight shoot of hazel or willow. Using natural bait from the streams or woods would be the most successful method.

Almost any stream has a great deal of aquatic life under its rocks, and one has only to turn these rocks carefully and gather the small insects. With a small bait on the hook, sink it carefully in a deep pool, taking extreme care when approaching a pool and presenting the bait. Any sudden movement drives the fish under the rocks or to other places of refuge.

Another good bait is found in rotten logs or stumps in the form of white grubs or termites. Even black ants would be good. A red huckleberry makes a fair salmon egg.

The majority of our small mountain streams have fish in their headwaters. Sometimes the stream will not be more than three or four feet wide, yet it will hold small trout. Various mountain lakes will also produce fish. You might have to resort to leaving a line out all night. This is not a legal means to fish, but in an emergency it should be permissible.

Many streams or inlets of lakes are so small that one can catch fish with his hands. Sometimes a small dam across the stream would trap the fish in a pool. Once I sent one of my young sons out to help a visiting boy catch some fish in a little brook near camp. When they returned they had a beautiful catch of brook trout. On inquiring how they caught them, I was told that they damned the stream in several places and caught them all with their hands. They were just as proud as though the fish had been taken on hook and line.

Another source of food from streams or lakes is crayfish. To catch them, lift the rocks in the bed of the stream carefully and grab them before they run. This same technique can be used on bullhead or catfish. A starving person might even eat the insect life found in a stream. Hellgrammite soup or caddis fly dip might make a passable hors d'oeuvres.

Other possibilities for food from streams would be frogs or turtles. The lakes in the high mountains are teeming with tadpoles, and sometimes the meadows are literally crawling with young frogs.

# AMPLE FOOD IN WILDS

Tonight we will sit down to an evening meal entirely from the wilderness. The first course will be mushroom soup, followed by a consomme of lichens. For salad we will have miner's lettuce spiced with a few sprigs of watercress.

Next we will roast some acorns or chinquapin nuts in the fire, and dessert will be a variety of berries, either fresh or dried. For a drink there is a choice of birch tea or a brew made from chicory.

An ample supply of food can be found in the woods, if you have the knowledge to identify it. Primitive man had to sample all the plants and finally settle on those that were edible and available. But present day man can find any amount of information on wild edible plants, and that information might mean the difference between starving and sustaining life.

Several factors would dictate what kinds of foods are available. The geographic location would be important, as well as the season of the year. Summer time, with all the green plants in full leaf and many ripe berries, would be an easy time. Other seasons might be more difficult.

Some people advise watching the animals and eating what they eat, but this is not always wise. Squirrels can eat the strong seeds of conifers or mushrooms that would be deadly to a human. Birds eat juniper berries, but all a man can stand is a little flavoring in his drink.

In the woods of Oregon a great many wild berries are found. To name a few: salal, blackberry, wild strawberry, thimbleberry, huckleberry, salmonberry, elderberry, gooseberry, wild raspberry, wild currant, and the favorite food of bears, the manzanita and bearberry. Many of these fruits were gathered and dried by the Indians to be pounded up later and added to soups or pemmican.

The Indians dug fern roots and roasted them in the fire. The white inner material was like starch. Another of their staple foods was camas root, and one found growing in the desert was Indian potato. Both are sweet little tubers that can be eaten raw or roasted. Acorns are greatly improved by heat; raw they are quite bitter, but roasted and pounded into flour they are very nutritious.

One of the most common plants in the deep woods is oxalis, sometimes called sorrel. This has a slightly sour taste and is a good addition to any salad. In the spring the tender tips of bracken fern can be eaten, as well as young nettles and the roots of horsetail or rush. Wild mustard is still picked for greens, and some people try lamb's quarter or pigweed. Dandelion greens can be used and sometimes fireweed which is so abundant in burned-over areas. When the leaves are dried they make a passable tea, and the young stems can be eaten like asparagus.

In the desert country almost all cactus is edible. Water can be obtained by cutting into the center of the plant. The flesh can be eaten raw, boiled or roasted.

Probably one of our most abundant foods is lichen or rock tripe. When boiled it becomes a thick gelatinous soup. Another food which is always available is the cambium layer of many different trees. The black bears know this. In the spring they peel off the outer bark to find the tender inner bark of firs, alder, maple and willow.

# CHAPTER II

# SEASONS AND OTHER PLEASURES

*Therefore all seasons shall be sweet to thee,*
*Whether the summer clothe the general earth*
*With greenness, or the redbreast sit and sing*
*Betwixt the tufts of snow on the bare branch*
*Of mossy apple-tree, while the nigh thatch*
*Smokes in the sun-thaw; whether the eave-drops fall*
*Heard only in the trances of the blast,*
*Or if the secret ministry of frost*
*Shall hang them up in silent icicles,*
*Quietly shining to the quiet moon*

*Samuel Taylor Coleridge (1772-1834)*

# WOODLANDS WAKE

The little squirrel had been curled up in a tight ball in his warm nest in the old rotten log. For four months he had been motionless in the long sleep of hibernation. As the warmth of a returning spring touched the land, he began the first stirrings of his return to active life.

The coming of spring to the valleys of the Cascades is a gradual thing. It may start as early as a sunny week in January, when the first blooms of the grouse flower may be found. By February a frog or two can be heard, pink catkins are dangling from bare alder branches, and pussywillows are popping out everywhere. By March the skunk cabbage is coming out and the chorus of frogs is much louder. Even though there will be more cold weather, or even occasional snow, the signs of spring are unmistakable.

The first shrub to come out in the lowlands is the oso or Indian plum. It is followed by wild strawberry and anemone, and soon the first white trillium appears. As the days become longer and the sun warmer, all plant life begins budding and strange stirrings occur within the forest floor.

The animals sense the change in season even more rapidly than man. With the melting of the snow, deer and elk leave their wintering grounds and follow the snow line as it recedes, bringing them closer to their summer feeding areas. They frequent the south hill slopes and rocky ridges, where the ground is already bare and some browsing available.

Black bears are stirring, but have not left their dens. They must wait for their food supply to be ready. When they first come out, they feed on vegetation such as green grass and skunk cabbage. Foxes and coyotes are beginning a search for dens. Their young will be born in late spring.

It is a time of year when the male cougar roams the mountains in search of a mate. He may cover as many as 25 miles in a single night, passing up deer and elk herds carelessly, as he yields to his age-old instincts.

Woodpeckers are sending staccato messages on dry snags, while the blue grouse hoots from a tall fir tree, and the ruffed grouse starts drumming from his favorite log. The yellow hammer, or red-shafted flicker, is back and his calls echo through the woods.

Spring is also manifested in the aquatic life of streams. Insects that have been crawling around on the bottom in the larva stage all winter hatch into flies. This increased activity in insect life wakes the fish up. They start to feed and to run upstream to spawn. Likewise, the great chinook salmon, the king of them all, leaves the ocean to begin his search for spawning grounds.

The appearance of newly arrived birds, chipmunks and squirrels chattering and scolding in their forest, all signify the return of warm days and the beginning of a new growing season.

# BUG HATCHES ON A FISHING STREAM

In the evening when the first shadows fall on the river, one will notice many insects flying over the water. This is the magic hour the fly fisherman has been waiting for. All day the sun has been too bright and hot for these delicate insects to hatch. They must have the cool shade of an evening or a cloudy day.

What the fisherman sees is the adult fly that has just hatched from a nymph or underwater crawler. For perhaps one, two, or three years, depending on its kind, the insect has lived under the water; first in the egg stage, then the nymph or larvae stage. Most of its life span is spent in the water, crawling on the bottom of the stream and living under the rocks and moss.

The transformation into the adult stage takes a day or two, or perhaps a few hours, during which time the adult mates and lays its eggs. The eggs are laid in the water and sink to the bottom to begin the life cycle over again.

These are the flies that cause the trout to feed on the surface. A fly fisherman imitates the insect with an artificial fly tied nearly the same size and color.

These aquatic insects are divided into three main families: the may flies, stone flies and caddis flies. They supply most of the food in a trout stream. Each family of flies is characterized by the position of their wings.

The may flies are probably the best known and are identified by their translucent upright wings and a three-forked tail. They hatch in the water from a six-legged crawler. Many different colors and sizes are prevalent in the may fly family.

The stone fly hatches from a fast moving nymph that crawls out on the bank and sheds its skin. The dry shells will be noted clinging to rocks and branches. They are recognized by their wings folded scissor fashion over their backs.

The caddis flies hatch from a tiny case or tube. They leave the case in the water and emerge as an adult. Their wings are folded tent fashion over their backs.

The next time you are fishing on a stream, watch for the bug hatch. It is a secret that might mean the difference between success and failure.

# MAY FLY'S LIFE CYCLE

Not a ripple broke the surface of the pool. A swarm of midget insects droned over the white water. A kingfisher rattled a half-muted warning from his perch on a dead tree above the water. The time was early afternoon, the magic hour for the fly fisherman.

Suddenly there was the swirl and splash of a large trout. In a few moments another trout rose, higher up the pool. In five minutes the pool was dotted with rising fish. It was the beginning of the may fly hatch.

All year the tiny crawlers had hidden under the rocks in the bed of the stream, feeding on the plant life and not daring to venture far afield. Now it was their time to hatch, mate and lay eggs for next year's generation of may flies.

A may fly begins with an egg dropped into the water by its parent. The egg sinks to the bottom of the stream and hatches into a tiny crawler, visible at first only under a magnifying glass. The crawler, now called a may fly nymph, lives under and in the crevices of the smooth rocks. Its food is the one-celled plant life found in the bed of all good trout streams. This substance is what makes the rocks so slick when one is wading. The plant life, in turn, is nurtured by the cold water and sunlight that penetrates to the bottom.

The may fly nymph can be recognized by a three-pronged tail, which may be visible only under a glass. As the little crawler grows, it must be constantly aware of its enemies—other carnivorous crawlers, as well as many different kinds of fish.

In the may fly family there are many different sizes, ranging from a quarter of an inch to large ones an inch in length. And the colors may vary from bright yellow to almost translucent pinks. A fly fisherman understands this and ties his imitations accordingly. In the process of hatching, the insect comes to the surface of the water, emerges from its nymphal skin, dries its gossamer wings and flies away as an adult. This is called the dun stage, and, when the insects are still on the water, the fish rise to feed on them. When the adult fly hatches, it has no alimentary canal and thus can take no food. Its only purpose is to procreate and disseminate the eggs.

Soon the slow flying adult will go into the woods where an amazing transformation will take place. It will shed another skin and emerge as a much more streamlined and active fly. Mating takes place in the air, and soon the female is laying her eggs on the surface of the stream. As the insect dips down to the water, barely touching the surface, she deposits a tiny egg which immediately sinks. The life cycle goes on.

# CADDIS BUILDS A HOUSE

The next time you are fishing on some lovely clear, cold stream, take time to sit down beside the water and watch intently for the little moving creatures on the bottom of the stream. Suddenly, you will see a stick moving. Or it may be a bit of sand and gravel. This will be the larva of the caddis fly. He will be crawling over the rocks, taking his little house with him.

Among the many aquatic insects found in our lakes and streams, the caddis flies form the largest group. They are also the largest contributor to the diet of the bottom feeding fish. The little crawler, as you see it on the bottom, is only one stage in the life cycle of the insect. A caddis fly is recognized by the wings, which are folded back over his body like a tent.

From an egg laid on the surface of the water the preceding summer, a little worm-like creature emerges and immediately starts building a house to live in. This is done by the accretion of many tiny particles adhering to the insect as he crawls. The house may be built of wood, or more often of small rocks and grains of sand.

The finished house is a little tube closed at one end. The larva puts his legs out of his house to crawl around over the stones and gather food. It withdraws them at the first sign of danger. As the tiny insect grows, so does his house. This is a mysterious part of his life cycle. How can he lengthen and widen his chamber and still remain inside?

Caddis cases, as they are now called, can take several shapes and sizes, from inch-long tubes of sand and gravel to square cases of material produced by the animal itself. Some, found in the high mountain lakes, are constructed from chewed particles of grass.

Seeing the insect at this stage, it is hard to imagine that some day, at the completion of his life cycle, he will be a beautifully colored fly darting through the trees on the stream's bank and skimming over the water in erratic flight. When the time to hatch comes, the little crawler goes under a rock or piece of wood on the stream bottom and seals himself to the object. This is called the pupa stage, and here a great transformation takes place. Wings start to grow, and the entire insect begins to take the shape of a fly. Emerging from the pupa stage, he sheds a thin, transparent skin and flies away as a mature caddis fly. His purpose now is to mate and disseminate eggs over a wide area of the parent stream.

The insect flies erratically over the water surface, with occasional dips to touch the water and lay its eggs. The microscopic eggs will sink to the bottom, where they hatch into larvae.

During adulthood the caddis fly takes no food, and his life expectancy ranges from a few hours to a day or two. With the laying of eggs completed, he is now a spent fly and will fall on the water to float downstream and perhaps be taken by a hungry trout.

Experienced fly fishermen will take note of the color and shape of the adult caddis fly and try to tie an imitation. One of the most unusual caddis flies is a decidedly green one found on the McKenzie River—hence the name "Green McKenzie."

# RUNNING THE DESCHUTES

We had that wonderful feeling of approaching adventure. With two boats launched in the river and duffle stored in the proper places, we were embarking on the first known river running of the Deschutes in Central Oregon.

The time was 1929, and river running in that era was almost unknown. Boats were of the old type McKenzie design with low sides and wide plank bottoms. This was before waterproof plywood was invented.

For several years we had fished the Deschutes River and traveled along its banks, each time wondering what was in some of the inaccessible canyons. Now we were launched on a trip down the entire river to its confluence with the Columbia. Our starting point was Grandview Bridge, a few miles upstream from where the Deschutes was joined by the Crooked River.

The river here was narrow but quite deep. Small rapids were throwing white water from the submerged boulders, but as far as we could see downstream, the way was clear. We had prepared well for this trip, even to the extent of planning to sleep in our boats if the rattlesnakes got too thick. We had heard tales of the river banks just crawling with snakes, and there was the possibility of not finding adequate space to camp in some of the narrow canyons.

The first mile was a nice little river with fish rising in the deep pools. Great rock cliffs walled the narrow valley so there was only room for the river. This was typical of many of the desert rivers of Eastern Oregon, where the streams had cut themselves a path through the high, ancient volcanic plateau. Sheer walls of basaltic columns rose hundreds of feet on both sides, and the talus slope from these eroding rocks extended to the water's edge.

We had traveled perhaps two miles when, upon rounding a turn in the river, we saw a tree blocking the channel. This necessitated a portage and a most difficult job of pulling the boats up over the tree and back into the water. This is one of the hazards of river running. One must always be on the alert for an obstacle blocking the stream, a falls, or a rapids that is impossible to run.

Each turn in the stream presented a wildly beautiful picture. Little streaks of foam trailed downstream from submerged rocks. Quiet pools held the promise of rainbows waiting for any insect that would light on the surface. A thin fringe of willows and alders fenced the stream in its narrow channel, and many kinds of birds flitted back and forth across the water in search of the insects that were hatching from its clear depths. In this desert country the streams are the focal points for all the birds and animals.

Rounding another sharp turn in the river, we were confronted with a second log across the channel. This one was in a narrow swift place which made it difficult to stop in time. By grabbing bushes and holding on, we managed to stop.

Then we let the boats down, one at a time, to the log where we could lift them over. This meant unloading the boats and carrying the baggage around—a critical move for me, because one of the boys fell and dropped my bedroll in the river. We didn't have the boats available, so all we could do was watch it float out of sight. We thought the bedroll would drift into some pool and stop, but this was not the case.

For the rest of the trip, I had to sleep rolled up in a small tent.

The canyon had been getting narrower and narrower all afternoon, and shale slides came to the water's edge, leaving no beaches for a camp. But after another mile, we spotted a big flat rock where we could cook and perhaps precariously roll up in our sleeping bags. In spite of limited space, we spent a good night lulled to sleep by the music of the stream.

A canyon in the desert always awakens early. At daybreak the birds begin to sing, kingfishers rattle as they pass over camp, and some curious magpie calls to his friends to come see what he has found. In this cacophony of sounds one is urged to get up.

That day we had some tough water by standards of river runners. Some of the rapids had to be scouted before running, and others were so rough that one man was kept busy bailing.

By noon we had come to the mouth of Crooked River. With more water and fewer rocks, we thought our bad water was behind. But with the Metolius River joining three miles downstream, we had a big river. Our problem now was to avoid the extremely high waves.

A white sandy beach invited us to stop for lunch, so while one man built a fire, the others started to fish. In a few minutes we had six wriggling rainbows in the sand. These fish were almost purple from living in the dark waters of the canyon.

This was a fisherman's paradise. Midday, when the insects hatched, the water's surface was constantly broken by rising fish. Many of these pools had never been fished.

For miles and miles the canyon was almost inaccessible, unless one wanted to hike from the canyon's rim to the river 2,000 feet below. Along the river, in the juniper trees, the ospreys had built numerous nests. They appeared as huge piles of sticks in the forks of trees. Occasionally a nest would be built on top of a rock pinnacle. In the higher rims we could see hawks' and eagles' nests. Our intrusion brought them out with their warning cries.

One side of the river was Indian reservation, and that day we saw an Indian on his horse outlined against the sky. He watched us until we were out of sight and probably wondered about the vagaries of the white man.

The second night we camped on a low flat sand bar that seemed the ideal camp but which almost brought disaster later. After the evening meal, we examined the surrounding country looking for Indian artifacts and the signs of birds and animals. Then, in the growing darkness, we sensed that the river was rising rapidly.

Gathering camping equipment and retrieving the floating boats, we soon had camp moved to higher ground and once more settled down. We never did know what had caused the rising stream; probably a heavy rain in the upper valley. This experience taught me to always camp on high ground when near a stream.

The following days were spent floating downstream leisurely, fishing as the mood caught us and camping on little islands or sand bars completely void of the signs of man. The islands were a paradise for birds. Here they could nest away from predatory animals and have a supply of food handy in the form of aquatic insects hatching from the river.

On one of these islands we located a big horned owl's nest. Under the nest were the remnants of the birds and animals on which they preyed. The evidence showed ducks, rabbits, quail and many smaller birds. When it got dark. we called one of the owls over to camp where he alighted. This calling is accomplished by imitating as closely as possible the call of the owl, who is fooled into thinking that he has company.

On the fourth day we came to the famous White Horse Rapids. Stories indicated that this was a bad rapids and had never been run with a boat. Of course this was a challenge to us.

After looking it over for some time, we selected a route

through the middle. Big rocks were breaking the water everywhere with huge troughs and whirlpools below, but there were wide channels between them. Luckily we did not break any oars. I believe we were the first to run this rapids.

The next morning we planned to get an early start. In the cold gray light of early morning we were standing around the fire warming our hands and drinking coffee. Suddenly I heard the unmistakable sound of a rattlesnake. It sounded like dropping coarse sand on a dry newspaper. Our fire had disturbed this unfriendly inhabitant who was coiled under a nearby sagebrush. Since then we have had many encounters with rattlesnakes, but without an accident other than a badly frightened dude.

Several other rapids followed White Horse, with such ominous names as Wapinita Falls, Roaring Springs, and Kicking Mule. All of them had a passage through. A portage had to be made at Shearer Falls, as it was impossible to run.

From this narrow gorge to the Columbia we had many white-water rapids, but none as bad as the one just at the mouth of the river where the road crossed it. This was where we planned to take out.

As there was a large crowd on the bridge waiting for us to show up, we knew we had to run this last rapids. After looking it over for an hour or more, we finally decided on a way through. It looked possible, but we knew that this would be the toughest rapids of the trip.

We made it with both boats, but each boat had taken on plenty of water. Drifting into the sluggish Columbia, we realized we had been the first to conquer the treacherous lower Deschutes.

# JOHN DAY RIVER TRIP

For several years our group of river adventurers had planned a river trip on some new stream. This year it was the John Day River of Central Oregon. We had just returned from an exploratory trip of 45 miles from Service Creek to Clarno.

Seven McKenzie boats with 14 passengers pushed off. The boats were loaded with personal duffel and food for four days. Among the passengers were a doctor and his wife, a banker and his wife, a sporting goods manufacturer, a 69 year old woman from Tacoma and several guides.

The people's interests in taking the trip were as varied as the personnel. Some were going for fishing, some for pictures, some for a collection of rocks, and one man had a Geiger counter. Regardless of their individual interests, they all had one in common—the spirit of adventure. All wanted to see what was around the next bend.

The John Day River is typical of the small desert rivers of Eastern Oregon. Flowing in a deep canyon most of the way, it is at times as picturesque as the Grand Canyon. Great black cliffs of columnar basalt extend to the water's edge. A cross section of the desert plateau made by the river shows successive lava flows of a past geologic period. Between these lava flows will be found colorful beds of sedimentary rock deposited by the ancient inland seas. It is here that many fossils of a tropical climate are encountered.

It is paradise for the geologist. Here will be a colorful

mountain of sandstone or limestone, capped by a lava flow to keep it from eroding. A great fault will be exposed by the river. A basaltic dike will turn the river's course into the opposite bank. Basaltic columns will appear as a huge pile of fence posts.

Along the banks of the stream will be found the typical vegetation of the desert. Sagebrush and juniper make up most of the plant life, but willows, wild roses and small brush create dense thicket near the water's edge. Some of the wildflowers, such as lupine, desert primrose and wild sunflower, were just beginning to bloom.

The first day we made about eight miles and stopped to camp at a little stream called Shoo-Fly Creek. Everybody jumped from their boats and began to unload baggage and make camp. The thoughts of big juicy steaks and buttermilk biscuits hastened their preparations.

Just at daylight we were awakened by a noisy coyote chorus. They like to tune up as the night gives way to daylight and they come in from the hunt. From then on the birds took over. It was like a great city coming to life. The songs of many birds filled the air. It was beautiful music to the ears of people fresh from the city.

In an arid region like the John Day Valley, all the birds like to nest along the river. Red winged blackbirds, meadow larks, western tanagers and many other smaller birds were seen, as well as doves, quail, pheasants, ducks and geese. The low green islands and grassy banks are wonderful nesting grounds for Canadian honkers. We saw several hundred each day, as well as numerous pairs with their young.

As we drifted down the river, the wise honkers knew the danger was coming from the water, so they and the young brood would take to the sage brush. Making themselves as small as possible as they reached the bank, they would all disappear in the tall brush along the stream.

The cliffs and caves along the river were great places for

ospreys, hawks and owls to nest. We climbed up to one osprey nest of sticks on a high pinnacle and collected one of the three eggs in the nest. It was as large as a big hen egg with brown and green splotches. In another place near our second camp, we noted a red-tailed hawk's nest with three downy white youngsters. The old birds would hunt upon the high plateau and then come swooping down to the nest with their prey in their claws. The young hawks would set up a clamor that we could hear for several hundred yards.

In another spot near camp, we found the nest of the great hoot owl with two young. They were just getting over the downy stage and were beginning to fly. Under the nest were the remains of their feasts. We identified rabbits, quail, ducks, snakes and several small birds.

Towards the end of the second day it began to rain, so we started looking for a good camping place. For a party that size it took quite a bit of space. Wood was the important thing, with the possibility of shelter second. We all had tents or tarps to stretch, and some of the guides would turn over their boats and sleep under them. After drifting downstream an hour or two, we spotted a good camping place at the base of a small cliff. It was overhanging just enough to set up a table in the dry. In a few minutes we had a roaring fire going some 15 feet from the cliff. Those wanting to dry out or get warm would get in near the cliff, and the reflection was like a huge fireplace.

Once again we got out the big dutch oven and started dinner preparations.

The third day of our river trip down the John Day took us past Burnt Ranch, where we stopped to talk to one of the old-timers of this region. He had lived there for 53 years and remembered when the Indians had burned the old original buildings on the ranch, thus earning this name of Burnt Ranch. His cordial invitation to come back and deer hunt in that country started us planning another trip.

The next day down the river was one of constant exploration. Every cave was visited by someone looking for fossils, rocks, or Indian artifacts. Every inviting canyon was tramped a mile or two. Rattlesnake Canyon lived up to its reputation by one of the boys killing a big denizen. By this time some of the boats were getting pretty well loaded with rock specimens, queer pieces of driftwood, and "white man" artifacts picked up around some of the abandoned homesteads.

Old tumbled-down shacks along the river showed where, in the early days, settlers had tried to make homes. Attempts had been made with all kinds of contrivances, from water wheels to homemade pumps, to get water on the land. With modern electric or gasoline pumps, it might have been a different story.

The last night out brought rain again. We made camp in the junipers along the stream. Everything seemed to be snug and ready for the night until someone suggested we all go up to a big cave in the cliffs above camp and sleep there. So at bedtime everybody gathered up air mattresses and sleeping bags and hiked up the mountainside several hundred feet to the cave. It was an ideal place to camp. Dry and protected from the wind, it commanded a beautiful view up and down the river.

We were not the only occupants of the cave. Numerous swallows were roosting in the niches among the rocks. The next morning one of the boys picked up one of the little birds. It seemed to be in an almost dormant state until he had handled it awhile and woke it up. The amazing thing was that all the birds were roosting with their heads facing back into the little rock niches.

We were awakened by the voices of many birds. The big cave was like an enormous ear located above the valley floor. It picked up the cackling of old China roosters, the calling of doves, quail and ducks. The sun came out, and we prepared to spend our last day on the river. We drifted 10 or 12 miles farther down and saw a few people, but lots of wildlife as before. Our cars met us at Clarno, where a bridge crosses the John Day.

Part of the value of these trips lies in the ability to make life seem longer. A weekend spent at home with routine activities soon passes and is forgotten, but the experiences which one may crowd into three or four days on some new river makes that period of time memorable. These pleasures of exploration and adventure are easily within the reach of anyone who is willing to overlook a few minor discomforts in order to enjoy them.

His reward will be in sights and sounds denied the ordinary individual. He will hear the call of the great Canadian honker or float some wild beautiful stream, see the golden crescent of the moon among rugged cliffs, and experience the warmth and companionship of friends around an evening campfire.

# BLITZEN RIVER

A river man is constantly on watch for some good river to float. This led to the discovery and planning of a trip down the Blitzen, a small desert river rising in the Steens Mountains of Southeastern Oregon and emptying into Malheur Lake.

From all the information we could get from the local residents, the river was not bad—no rough white water reported and just a nice little shallow river. However, there were some 15 miles of stream they were rather vague about.

To a spot where we could launch the boats necessitated a drive of some 30 miles over the desert in a power wagon. The road was not much more than a buckaroo trail. Arriving at the river, we pumped up the boats and stored duffle aboard. We had a four-man and a seven-man boat equipped with wooden frames and good stout oars.

The river looked nice where we started. One could wade it almost any place. This was a celebrated fishing stream lower down, and we could see an occasional fish rising in the big pools. They were surprisingly big for such a small stream. Fish up to a pound were common. The first half mile was a nice little stream with a few rapids and wide shallow riffles. Then suddenly things changed. The river was dropping in more of a canyon and getting much swifter. The canyon had narrowed, and huge boulders blocked its passage. The rapids were getting worse, and by the second mile we were lining many of them. In a few places we would have to take the boats out of the water and slide them over the big boulders.

The first afternoon we made only three miles, and the river was getting steadily tougher. The canyon was getting so narrow that we had a bad time just finding a place to camp. Finally at 6:00 we found a series of little sand patches behind big rocks where a man could sleep. In the morning we hiked out of the canyon to see if there was any possibility of getting horses down to the river. If so, we were going to pack out and abandon the trip. We found there was no chance of getting horses to the river, so we launched the boats again.

In the first two hours we floated only a half mile and could look back and see the previous night's camp. Then the canyon opened into a wide valley. We thought we had it made, and so set up rods and had some fine fishing. After a few miles the canyon narrowed once more, and we had the bad rapids all over again. My companion broke two oars, and we had to make a spare out of a piece of the boat frame and the top of a small juniper.

That day we made only five miles, and again we hiked out of the canyon to see if it were possible to get horses to the river. It was too rough and rocky, so we knew we had to complete the trip or leave everything and walk out. It was a matter of floating only a few hundred feet and then portaging or lining again. This continued for the third day, and, by that time, we were getting short on food.

On the fourth day, about noon, I noted the first sign of any human having been in the canyon. It was the stump of an old juniper, probably cut 75 years before. In a short distance I noticed another stump and deducted that this could only mean one thing. Someone had hiked up the canyon and cut posts to float down the river to the ranches in the valley. If this were the case, as it later proved, we would soon strike better going. Through much of the canyon we had traversed they could not have floated big posts down the river.

From this time on the stream improved to the point where we knew we had it made. A landmark told us it was only a few more miles out, so we set up rods again and had some of the finest fishing I have ever seen.

It was a perfect stream now, about 50 feet wide, with big pools every so often. Fish were rising everywhere to a hatch of blue uprights. Soon the canyon opened to the valley, and we knew the trip was over.

# A DRIFT TRIP ON THE ROUGE

With the coming of early fall, the great run of steelheads enter the mouth of the Rogue River on their annual migration up the river to spawn. This is the time of year when many fishermen make the boat trip through the wilderness area of the Rogue from Grants Pass to Gold Beach.

The boats are launched, and the 60 mile trip of lovely wilderness lies ahead. This trip will take four days. Nights are spent camping on the gravel bars or staying at the lodges maintained especially for the river adventurers.

No sooner do the boats get underway, when the first white water shows in the distance. From then on there will be many rapids and, in addition, one falls that must be portaged. The degree of danger in the rapids is soon manifested by the numerous wrecked boats lying along the shore. This is a river for the experienced only. Each summer many boats are capsized and some lost by the river runners. People come from all over the United States to try their luck or skill on the Rogue.

In early afternoon, as soon as the shade reaches a good riffle, the rods are set up and fishing begins. This is the thrill that many have been waiting for. There is no greater fish for fighting qualities and fast action than a steelhead. The strike is fast and hard, and it may be 20 minutes until the hooked fish is landed.

Most of the "dudes" making this trip with a guide are novices in fishing, and one can imagine the excitement of hooking the first fish. With the landing of the fish, it is now time to find a good spot for lunch. Grilled steelhead with a little salt, butter and lemon juice is fit for a king. Just as the fish finishes browning over the hot coals, a handful of green willow is added to smoke it for a few minutes.

By late afternoon the shadows are falling in the deep canyon, and it is time to think about making camp. It is also time for the bears to come out on their evening patrol of the stream banks, in hopes of finding a salmon. Quite a number of salmon die in their spawning migration and float downstream. In a deep stream like this, the bears can seldom catch their own.

On every early fall trip we see from one to five black bears. They have plainly marked trails up and down the banks, where they travel nightly to seek a salmon that has drifted into the shore.

On the last trip we saw a big black bear coming slowly up along the river. As he climbed over a rock ledge, his belly came into contact with the rough rocks. This felt so good that he remained there for a minute or so scratching himself on the rocks.

The rapids and fishing have been so exciting that little time has been spent admiring the scenery. In all of Oregon there is no more rugged or beautiful sight. Great walled canyons enclose the river in narrow gorges. A river 200 feet wide will be crammed down a solid rock shoot not more than 20 feet wide.

The erosion of centuries is depicted in the solid black basalt. Weird figures have been carved by the sand and gravel of past floods. The rock walls near the water have been worn smooth and shiny, but, above the highwater mark, a great variety of shrubs and trees cling to the precipitous sides.

This is where the northern and southern plant life meet. Douglas firs are mixed with Ponderosa pines, and rhododendrons give way to azaleas. California Bay trees appear in high groves, and four species of oaks grow on the dry hillsides.

Madrone trees with their lovely smooth brown bark line the river banks, while the first Port Orford cedars appear as we near the coast.

It is a country of much wild game. Besides the deer and bear, other animals such as coyotes, lynx cats and cougars, leave their tracks on the sand bars. Almost every steep bank has its otter slide, and we frequently see a family of river otters fishing or playing near the water.

They are the most playful and affectionate of all animal families. With a shrill chirp of "follow me," they dive and swim, chasing each other through the deep pools. Occasionally they come up from a dive with a fish in their mouths. The fish is usually a trash fish such as a chub or sucker, but sometimes they catch a salmon or steelhead. Then the whole family climbs up on a rock to dine. Wild pigeons feed on the acorns of the oak trees; flocks of crows wander on a sand bar; a covey of mountain quail will come down to the water's edge, and a lonely great blue heron will stand motionless in the shallows waiting for a fish to swim by. Mergansers and wood ducks line the stream. They are seldom disturbed, except by a passing boat.

Early morning mists rise from the river as the first fishing of the day begins. The air is crisp with the chill of fall in the air. The boats drift almost soundlessly down into steelhead water.

As the deep rugged canyon cuts through the coast range, the mountains give way to more rounded hills covered with heavy timber. The geological formations change. From a canyon of solid rock, one now enters a sedimentary rock area. Conglomerate gravels, sandstone and shale appear. There is evidence of an ancient lake or river bed. A faint touch of ocean breeze reaches up the river, and a few seagulls appear.

The river becomes less turbulent, and the first signs of civilization are at Illahee. After three days of wilderness, one is coming back to the world of motors and men. The Rogue River has been run, but pleasant memories of remote riffles and gravel bars remain.

# NATURE AT HER BEST

Take a day in June for just enjoying Nature at her loveliest. Find a place where you can know the warmth of the early-morning sun, the calling of birds and perhaps the murmur of a little stream. Try to shut out all sounds of civilization and all thoughts pertaining to the mechanics of living.

Know again and marvel at these things: the soft green of new hemlock cones, the tight curls of young fern fronds, the courage of baby robins on their first flight.

While on such a trip, one may have the chance to see interesting and unusual sights in nature. I can recall seeing a number of almost unbelievable sights while camped out in some secluded spots. One morning, as we were getting breakfast near Rebel Rock in early spring, we were amazed to see black bears playing in the snow just like children. A mother bear slid down a small incline, chest down and paws outspread. Her cubs watched this with great interest; then as she came to the top and slid down again, they also began to play this game, which kept up until the mother ambled off into the brush.

Another odd episode occurred near a lookout. A yellow hammer or flicker had found a piece of tin to sound out his messages. This resounding noise had attracted all the flickers nearby.

An interesting sight on the river is the variety of birds catching insects to feed their young. The swallows are the signalmen for the other birds, and when they start swooping over the stream, they are soon followed by the western tanager, blackbirds, robins, the downy woodpecker, Audubon's warbler, and other small birds. It is amazing to see that the blackbirds can catch dozens of insects, adding one without dropping the rest, until their heads are bristling with the bugs. Finally, they leave the water and feed their young in the nest.

If one is quiet in the woods, he may be rewarded by seeing something denied the usual traveler. One morning I was on a deer stand near a small stream where several deer trails merged. As I watched over a big forested valley, a cougar suddenly appeared. He jumped upon a log not a hundred yards in front of me and also began surveying the valley. He was sleek and graceful, and his long tail twitched occasionally. Perhaps his sixth sense warned him that some enemy was near. After a few minutes he jumped down from the log and disappeared.

There was another instance which I recall as an unusual sight. We were camped near a salt lick up South Fork. One evening, just at dusk, a cow elk came to the lick. She was followed by a young fawn who trailed along behind as if he were her own calf. We wondered about this odd relationship and how it had formed. No doubt the fawn had lost its mother, but had the elk also lost her calf, or was she one of those barren animals that never have young? We never knew the answers.

The seasons are all too short to see and enjoy the things which are waiting to be discovered. Take a trip soon and find out more about the adventure of wilderness.

# LINTON VALLEY CAMP

Our camp is situated in a lovely valley bright with wild flowers so profuse they make a thick carpet everywhere. On guard are the Three Sisters, still snowy from winter, their age-old glaciers nestling on their slopes. These peaks change color each hour of the day, and the red-rock formations of the South Sister are fascinating in the glow of sunset.

On our right is the Husband, a gray twin-coned mountain almost as high as the Sisters. The nearby slopes are green with alpine fir and mountain hemlock. Low huckleberry brush and green heather cover the open ground.

Standing on each side of our camp, mute evidence of long-ago fire, are tall snags with knobby irregularities and tufts of moss. Woodpeckers have honeycombed these tough old hemlocks with hundreds of black holes. Pattern and designs have been carved by wind and weather, until these bare poles resemble the totem poles of the Indian tribes of the north.

There are birds all around. We have seen or heard many kinds. The Clark's nutcracker and Stellar's jays are the noisiest. Numerous rufous hummingbirds claim the area across the little clear creek which rushes past our camp. We can only catch glimpses as they flash back and forth in their paradise of flowers.

We also have several camp pets. A pair of chipmunks live in a rotten stump close by, and they dart out to steal food when things are quiet. Two does come each evening. They are very curious and seem quite tame. Ordinary noise and voices around our evening campfire do not frighten them. We know they want salt, so we leave it out for them. After dark we often hear their soft footfalls around camp. They bed down on a small bushy butte near camp during the day.

On a bench near camp is a little secret lake. The first trees which outline its shores are clearly reflected in its depths. And, just before dark, the surface of the water is broken by the circles of rising fish.

This is a quiet and lovely place. Far from the haunts of man, no phone brings you suddenly from the depths of sleep, no blaring of sirens tears the night. Here in this lovely wilderness man finds himself in complete harmony with nature.

A crescent moon has been getting larger and staying longer with us each night. It goes down between the peaks of the Husband. While we are still in this valley it will be full, and we can enjoy its silvery radiance against a dark star-studded sky.

# TRIPS TO THE HIGH LAKES

Nestled like glowing jewels in the green timbered valleys of the Cascades are a number of beautiful high mountain lakes. One of the clearest lakes in the Cascades is Spring Lake. Drive to Frog Camp on the McKenzie Highway, then hike one mile up the Obsidian Trail, then a half mile on to the lake. This is a very deep lake and quite typical of those found in volcanic country.

Another short hike is into Linton Lake, which may be reached by driving to Lower Alder Springs, then taking a trail from there. A short two mile walk brings you to this beautiful little basin in a cove of the mountains at the base of the Middle Sister. It has a lovely waterfall coming in from the east side. German brown trout are present and will hit best at late evening or during cloudy weather.

Drive on up to Scott Lake on the same highway and take the trail from there to Benson Lake. This is a large, deep body of water stocked with rainbow trout. Note the glacial striations on the rocks just east of the lake.

A little farther on (one mile) will take you to Tenas Lakes. There are three small lakes in this group, all stocked with eastern brook trout.

Another interesting trip would be in a ten mile drive up South Fork, then a four mile drive up the Hardy Creek road to Hidden Lake. This lake, when first found by white man, was populated with a pure strain of cutthroat trout. This has been a popular fishing lake for many years, but the fact that it can now be reached by a road has cut down its fish population. Best fishing is always in a lake which is not so easily accessible.

One of the nicest trips of all is to drive to Skookum Creek at the head of the South Fork and hike into the Erma Bell Lakes. Otter, Mud, Williams, or any number of lakes farther south towards Waldo, are all good bets for fishing. This is one of the finest groups of lakes in Oregon. All are well stocked with trout, which usually bite best toward evening.

Another nice one day trip for the family is the Century Drive out of Bend. You can make this circle and visit several beautiful lakes, among them Todd and Sparks, as well as seeing some high alpine meadow country and snow peaks.

On any of these trips one should take along lunch, flies or lures for the fisherman, and long sleeved shirts and insect repellant for the whole family. Mosquitoes may not be bad everywhere, but it is a good idea to be prepared. And remember, any time spent in the woods or lake country is rewarding.

# HIGH MOUNTAIN LAKES

There is a fascinating story to be told of our high mountain lakes, their geological formation, and more recent development as areas for fishing and recreation.

In the last glacial period great masses of ice formed in the Cascades, then pushed down the mountain sides to the lower country. In this massive movement of millions of tons of ice and debris, the earth's surface was carved, gouged, and striated and little glacial lakes were formed. As a mass of ice would push over a ridge, it would dig at the foot of the steep incline and thus form a basin that would later fill with water. Even now one can see striations in the rocks near the lakes.

Today these lakes offer fine recreation for outdoor people. When the lakes were first discovered by white men, few of them held fish, but in recent years most all of the lakes of sufficient depth have been stocked by the State. The lakes are first examined to determine if they will support fish life, then a small drop is made from a plane.

Planting by plane is a fairly new practice. Until the late 1950's, lakes were stocked by pack horses, each carrying two cans of water with little fingerlings. This, of course, was slow work, and many of the tiny trout would die before reaching the lake. Now, in a few minutes, the trout may be loaded at the hatchery and flown into inaccessible lakes, to be dropped from a hundred feet or more so they can orient themselves and hit head first in the water. Almost one hundred percent survival is possible.

Lakes are stocked with several species of trout. Eastern brook are a favorite in rather warm lakes. Rainbows predominate in most plantings, but sometimes German browns are released. In recent years the beautifully colored golden trout have been stocked in some of the very high lakes. Some of the lakes between the Middle and South Sisters have these trout.

The growth of these fish depends on the temperature of the water and the food available. Sometimes aquatic life must be planted before the fish are placed in the lake. Fresh water shrimp and crawfish are a favorite food. However, most of the lakes already have a resident insect life sufficient to feed a limited number of fish. When a body of water is over-stocked, the fish will remain small with large heads and very slender bodies.

Another problem encountered in high mountain lakes is the winter kill. This is a condition caused by insufficient oxygen when the lake is frozen over. Sometimes one will come back to a little lake and find all the fish dead. Water must be of sufficient depth, and some flow of water into the lake is desirable.

Many mountain lakes must be stocked every few years, as they are unfavorable to the natural fish spawning. Trout must have running water in which to spawn. Sometimes this is made possible by small streams flowing in and out of lakes, and by underwater springs.

You may be near a lake when the restocking is done. A plane will come over, dive at the lake and a cloud of vapor will appear. Soon raindrops will dot the lake's surface—tiny trout diving into their future home.

# COLOR IN THE MEADOWS

Nature is lavish with her colors, especially in wild flowers. Picture a high mountain meadow in early summer with its Indian paint brush, lupine, monkey flower, larkspur and penstemon. Such a gaudy array of colors, yet they blend in perfectly.

By following the seasons to the higher elevations, one can find some kind of a wild flower almost any month of the year. Starting in January, the wild strawberry is blooming in the lower valleys. Soon the yellow violet and tiny grouse flower or blue bell come out.

February and March bring the trilliums, wild currants and spring beauties. And the earliest blooming shrub is oso, or Indian plum. By the first of May, the rhododendrons and dogwoods are in full bloom. One of the most precious little flowers to be found is the calypso orchid or lady slipper. It grows in the dense dark woods in heavy moss and only lasts a few weeks.

As summer progresses, the flowers start climbing the mountains. The same flowers that bloomed in the valley may be found a month later in the higher elevations. Here also, one will find flowers not known to the lower valleys. The mariposa lily or cat's ear growing in the dry sandy flats is a treasure. Snow-white snow lilies may also be encountered.

A rare prize is the Western anemone or "old man of the mountains." Note that there are almost always at least two names for the common flowers.

Along the cold mountain streams and in the meadows of the High Cascades, one will find floral arrangements untouched by man. An island in a little creek will be covered with lupine, shooting stars, Queen Anne's lace, penstemon, paint brush and marsh marigolds. No gardener could produce a rock garden so beautiful.

Even in the rock areas well above the timberline, lovely flowers grow. The mountain heather, both pink and white, growing on the bare rocks, and the tiny flowers of the pink alpine phlox clinging to the dry rock ledges, are present everywhere.

As one climbs from the lower valleys past the timberline, he passes through a number of life zones. Each zone has its characteristic plant life. Note the mountain lily, called Hood or Shasta lily, on the open hillsides. It will be intermingled with columbine, lupine, bear grass and one or more of the brightly colored penstemons. And don't forget the lovely blue polemonium, or mountain valerian. Polemonium, sometimes called Jacobs ladder, is quite rare, while valerian is common even along the valley streams.

If you gather a bouquet in a high mountain meadow, you can have twenty or thirty kinds of flowers. One of the most brilliant would be the rare farewell to summer. It is in this paradise of wild flowers that the little hummingbirds like to nest. As you invade their territory, the constant buzzing and darting almost at your face will let you know that a nest is near.

# FALL TRIP TO THE WOODS

Autumn brings many changes to the woods, streams and high mountain areas. One should take several fall trips just to appreciate these changes—to enjoy the beauty of fall colors, to see how the birds and animals respond to another season. The High Cascades, the Steens Mountains, the Rogue River all reflect a new time of year.

The mountain valleys, so bright with multi-colored wild flowers in spring and summer, are now ablaze with foliage which has turned brilliant after the first frosty nights. This brilliance is also due to the dryness of the season, as foliage does not necessarily need to wait for cold weather in order to achieve color. One of the most vivid shrubs in its fall dress is the wild blueberry bush, covering the ground in many places. This forms a red carpet for hillsides around high mountain meadows. In the valleys below, dogwood and vine maple bring their touches of pink and gold to the dark green forest canopy.

East of the Cascades one may find the brilliant yellow of willow and aspen. The area around Fish Lake and Fish Creek in the Steens Mountain region is especially beautiful and well worth a trip into that part of the state. While there, one may see thousands of migrating red-breasted robins stopping to feed on ripe juniper berries.

Summer actually lasts only a scant two months in some high elevations, as snow can come again in August. This year the first white powdery stuff fell in early September, and all the region around the Three Sisters got several inches. This was a warning storm for the animals, the first indication that summer was over and fall was on its way.

There is a strange unrest on the part of some wild animals in the fall and furious activity from others. Deer and elk move down from six or seven thousand feet, where they have summered, and go into the dense timber. The smaller animals, such as squirrels and coneys, are putting away food and preparing homes for the long winter ahead. The squirrel families are hiding huge caches of fir cones, maple seeds, and hazel nuts. These may be under fallen logs or in the crotches of trees, where they may be found after snow is on the ground. Coneys are bringing loads of dry grasses into their tunnels for winter use. Bears are putting on layers of fat to last them through their winter sleep.

The mountain lakes also change in the fall. Not a ripple stirs the surface of the lake, where there were dozens of rising fish at dusk in July and August. Instead, there may be a single beaver-chewed stick floating near the bank; or if one comes up quietly, a band of mallards or teal resting and feeding between stretches of their migration south.

The first Canadian honkers fly south in early September. On a clear windless night, these harbingers of fall give their wild and free calls. Another season, another year almost finished.

# SIGNS OF AUTUMN

A hike through the woods at this time of year can turn up many interesting stories. A keen observer can read the signs that unfold in the everyday life of the wild animals in their preparations for winter.

In a little timbered valley up the South Fork stands a hollow fir tree that has served as a bear's den for many, many years. Around this tree, on the nearby dogwoods and cedars, are found the claw marks of the past inhabitants. As each bear claims the den for his winter hibernation, he rears up on the nearby trees and leaves his claw marks as high as he can reach.

The hole at the base of the big fir has had to be enlarged several times for the growing occupants. The interior of the hollow tree is dry, and the bug dust and rotten wood have formed a soft bed. When the deep winter snows cover the ground, the bear settles in for a long undisturbed sleep.

As you walk through the woods these fall days, you will hear a constant recurring thump, thump, thump coming from a thicket. On investigating, you will find that the sound is fir cones falling from some tall tree. A pine squirrel is cutting his winter supply of food. For hours at a time, he will be scurrying all over the high branches of the trees cutting loose the cones. Then he will come down to the ground to gather them up and hide them somewhere for the winter. His caches will be in or under a rotten log, at the base of a big tree or buried in the soft needles. When the winter snows come, he will have a supply of food.

On a recent hunt, I was skirting a large meadow in the high mountains. A little wooded knoll near the meadow revealed the remnants of three snow geese. A coyote had sneaked up on the geese and retired to the knoll to enjoy his feast. The different ages of the feathered kills showed that this was a regular occurrence for the coyote. When the birds were migrating, they would stop in the meadow to feed or rest. The coyote, hearing them, knew it meant another easy meal.

Such are the lives of the animals in the woods; a constant struggle for survival, a constant search for food and an unceasing vigilance.

# FALL IN THE CASCADES

The first snow of the season had fallen in the high mountains, and the animals were getting ready for a hard winter. The last storm left up to six inches of snow above the timberline, but in two days it was all gone and summer weather again took over. While the snow was on the ground, nature revealed all her hidden population.

Snowshoe rabbit tracks crossed, squirrel paths led from tree to tree, and here and there were the tracks of a foraging marten.

A black bear was feeding in a blueberry patch, stopping occasionally to add a succulent mushroom to his diet. Deer and elk were also hunting for mushrooms in the heavy timber.

A set of closely spaced tracks told where a porcupine was waddling from tree to tree. He would live up in this high country during the winter, seeking shelter under big rocks and climbing trees for his foraging of bark and buds. And across a small meadow, an erratic line of tracks told of the passing coyote hunting mice or gophers.

It was an amazing experience to note all the birds and animals in the alpine country. Red-shafted flickers were calling everywhere, and their mingling with red-breasted robins on the ground indicated that they were also feeding on the berries.

In early morning and late evening, the lonesome call of the white-breasted nuthatch sounded throughout the woods, and at daybreak one could also hear the lovely bell-toned call of the varied thrush.

Near a rocky promontory, a red-tailed hawk took to the air carrying a long white stick in one claw. He flew up into an old weathered hemlock snag and held the stick for several minutes. I believe that when he was startled, he had made a grab for his catch (a squirrel) and had flown away with the stick.

On another high ridge a blue darter hawk glided silently by. He is probably the most efficient killer in all the woods. His terrific speed allows him to catch at will almost any bird or squirrel.

In a dark silent hemlock thicket, a huge owl floated by on noiseless wings. With the coming of day, he was looking for a thick tree in which to spend the sunlit hours.

One of the reasons for so many birds was the big crop of huckleberries, blueberries and tiny red huckleberries no larger than a small bead. Blue grouse would frequently flush from the ground where they had been feeding on the berries. Joining them in the feast was a flock of bank-tailed pigeons.

From the top of a noble fir, a pine squirrel was dropping cones, which would soon be gathered and hidden for the winter. Little chipmunks were busy everywhere feeding on the berries and gathering bits of mushroom. With the coming of winter they would hibernate, as would the black bears and whistling marmots.

This was a bird watcher's paradise. Tiny birds of many kind were flittering through the tree tops, moving too fast for identification. A "come" call would be given by some Oregon jay, and soon several birds would be seen coming through the trees to investigate man. A camp meant a handout for them.

A family of Stellar's jays were announcing the passage of some animal. The noisiest of all were the Clark's nutcrackers giving their raucous warning calls.

It was autumn in the High Cascades, the summer visitors were gone and winter would soon take over.

# NATURE PREPARES

As late fall approaches and an early snow storm indicates the coming of winter, a strange disquiet falls upon the animals of the high mountains. Each of the animals, in his own way, feels the urgency to prepare for winter. This manifests itself in many ways.

The squirrels increase their tempo of storing food. The beavers are busy all night cutting branches and trees. The bears are looking for a warm, dry place to hibernate. Many of the birds are leaving for the south, and the deer and elk are getting ready to migrate to the lower valleys.

But many of the animals and birds choose to remain and spend the winter in the deep snow. The snowshoe rabbit, with big hind feet, is especially equipped for the occasion. The red fox, marten and weasel are light enough to travel on top of the snow. Many of the birds find an abundance of seeds and insects in the heavy timber. Some of the animals, like the chipmunk, bear and whistling marmot, solve their winter problems by hibernating.

The deer and elk follow trails that have been used for centuries, down to the lower hills where they will winter on the south slopes. This is usually brushy country, many times with rocky cliffs, but away from the heavier timber. There they will tend to bunch up and make a yarding ground, if the snow gets too deep. This is accomplished by getting together in numbers and keeping runways open by constantly traveling them, thus forming a labyrinth of trails. The yarding ground may be only a few acres in size, but with trails leading in all directions through the brush in which the deer and elk feed. This way the animals can find an abundance of food even though the snow gets several feet deep.

Deer and elk are browsing animals, feeding on such shrubs as willow, chinquapin, snowbrush, madrona and vine maple. In times of deep snow, they will even eat the tips of hemlock branches.

Several times I have noticed small deer following a big elk. When the elk, with his long legs and huge weight, bends down a tree or tall bush to eat the tips of the branches, the deer goes around and eats off the top. This is a working agreement that the elk must consent to, because if he tried to chase the deer away, he would lose his bent-over tree.

With the coming of spring and the snow melting, the migrating animals again start moving, but this time upwards, following the snow line until they are again in their summering grounds.

# TRAPPING IN THE SNOW

Trapping in the high mountains in the wintertime calls for the utmost of skill and resourcefulness in a man. It is perhaps the most exciting of all outdoor occupations, because a mistake in judgment, or a bad fall, may mean death in a bleak wilderness where there is no one to know or care.

The person who travels the high mountain trails in the summer months when the meadows are green, game plentiful, the sun warm, and the air crisp and clear, may have only a vague idea how these same mountains can change in winter. The ground is snow covered, streams frozen over, with few sights or sounds of animal or bird life. When storms descend (which they can do very suddenly), the icy wind drives snow mercilessly before it. The air is thick with cold fog, rendering visibility practically zero. Trails and signs are hidden, and the whole area takes on the atmosphere of a totally unfamiliar country.

A man who traps alone in the snow combats a number of unseen enemies. Therefore he must have unusual ability along many lines. He must be able to take care of himself in a sudden storm and be able to find shelter and make a fire under adverse conditions. He must know where to find dry wood when the forests are dripping with moisture and how to orient himself if he becomes lost. He should be rugged and healthy and able to live on scant rations if necessary. He must have coolness and strength, as well as complete confidence in his ability to survive under conditions very unfriendly to man.

The occupation also calls for a high degree of skill in trapping animals and a complete knowledge of the habits and ways of the animals, to make this a profitable business. Most of the trapping done in the Cascade area is for marten, fox, ermine, and an occasional mink.

The final quality which a man must have is perhaps the most important of all. This is the ability to live alone in the wilderness. The solitude and loneliness become overpowering for some people, and they become victims of a queer ailment. One day, while examining a trap, a man may have the feeling that he is being watched. A quick look behind assures him that no one is about. He goes on with the business at hand. The feeling persists, and again he turns unexpectedly, only to confront a snow covered scene. When he goes back to his cabin he travels a little faster than usual, his enthusiasm for his work is gone, and the peacefulness and beauty of the country has been ruined for him.

A trapper would love to have the companionship of a dog, but the deep snow which the man covers on snowshoes makes traveling impossible for a dog. Most trappers encourage the small animals to come around the cabin for companionship. These small creatures help combat the loneliness of the long winter nights.

Sometimes even the most experienced trappers have accidents. Many years ago a trapper failed to return in the spring. He had spent the winter alone in the High Cascades. It was not until 20 years later that his body was found in a little thicket near Todd Lake. The mystery of his death has never been solved.

# WINTER CAMPING TRIP

There is something especially exciting about a wintertime camping trip. To provide oneself with a warm fire and a dry bed while the woods are dripping with icy moisture is a challenge. When you are seated in your lean-to with a roaring fire out in front and the steaks grilling over coals, there is a rewarding, rich satisfaction. You feel completely at peace with the world.

These moments come all too seldom in the lives of most of us; we relegate camping for summertime, unaware of how much fun it can be in winter under the proper conditions. All it really takes is some knowledge of how to dress, how to make a proper camp and how to build a good fire in rain or snow.

Let me tell you of an overnight trip made in February into one of the valleys in the Cascades. We planned to take light equipment and simple food, as everything was to be carried in our packboards. We took with us these essentials: two waterproof tarps, one for shelter and one for ground cloth; sleeping bags, axe, matches, flashlight, small grill (8 oz.), aluminum foil, stainless steel cups, spoons and pocket knives, and of course, food for four meals. We wore light, warm clothing and had waterproof boots with wool socks.

We drove about 20 miles. Even before leaving our car we caught glimpses of two bands of elk and saw a doe and fawn standing motionless among the firs. This gave promise of what we might hope to see on our trip.

We started to hike about 11 o'clock and struck off across a

logged-off unit that blackened the landscape, but we soon hit the trail up a narrow valley. Two water crossings were made. One was on a log jam, and the other was made on fallen single log which made on a slippery, precarious bridge negotiable only by the presence of a wire stretched about shoulder height.

We hiked for an hour along a good trail through the dense trees and mountain meadow country. The ground, which had never been disturbed by logging, was a soft sponge of needles and moss.

Soon after our noon stop for tea we came to a place in the trail which we will never forget. Off to our right and below us lay several meadows with dried and snow-flattened grasses which offer good winter feed for deer and elk. We spotted several elk feeding in the nearest meadow. They were unaware of our presence, as we dropped our packs and crept quietly from bush to bush for a better view. The herd consisted of two dark little calves and six or eight cow elk and yearlings. We watched them feed for several minutes.

At dusk we found a place to camp beside a little stream. Two old fir snags, remnants of the huge forest which once covered this area, furnished wood. Our plastic tarp was soon draped over a cord stretched between trees and fastened securely to the ground on all sides. With our blazing fire in front of this shelter, and tongues of flame piercing the darkness on all sides, we were well prepared for the rain which fell all night.

After we had a bough bed made and everything snug for the night, we grilled our steaks. With the addition of toasted French bread, carrot strips and fruit, this was a fine meal.

All night we heard the sound of the little stream running nearby and the dripping of rain, but we were dry and comfortable. It turned colder, and in the morning there was snow visible on the mountain across from camp. After breakfast we broke camp.

This trip into the secret wintering ground of the deer and

elk took us away from home only a little more than 24 hours. Yet this experience, with its rewarding sights of game, and the peace and solitude which one finds close to nature, will remain long in our memory.

# BIRDS OF THE WINTERTIME

In the summertime one will find a great many birds in the High Cascades, but, with the coming of fall and cold weather, many of them go south. Probably the jays and woodpeckers are the only birds that store food. The Stellar's or blue jay may hide a few hazelnuts or filberts, and the woodpecker will hide a few acorns in some old snag.

Not many birds have this tendency to put food away for the winter. They must depend on migrating to a warmer place. The remaining birds that spend the winter in the deep snow country are peculiarly adapted in some way to find food and withstand the cold.

The blue grouse will spend most of the winter in the heavy forest, living up in the trees and eating the buds and leaves of the fir. He needs only to come down to the ground for water.

Some of the tiny insect-eating birds, such as the kinglets, winter wrens, nuthatches and chickadees, will find their food in the bark and leaves of the big trees. A heavy snowfall means nothing to them. They will have both shelter and food that cannot be covered by snow.

The forest also produces great quantities of seeds in the cones. This is food for both birds and squirrels. The Clark's nutcracker, with his powerful wedge-shaped beak, can always find a cone. Occasionally severe storms may drive him to the lower elevations, but, for the most part, he prefers to live as high on the mountain as the trees grow.

The water ouzels will find their fare, as long as the streams are running. They live on aquatic insect life and dive and swim in the cold water, picking insect larvae from under the rocks and in the moss. Other water birds, such as the belted kingfisher and fish ducks, eat fish and find their food as long as the streams and lakes are free from ice.

Gliding through the dense forests on silent wings are the owls: the great horned owl, the pygmy owl and the spotted owl. Their food, consisting of birds, mice, rabbits and squirrels, is usually abundant. The deep resonant call of the bog hoot owl is well known to the forest wanderer.

These birds are companions to the lonely trapper in the wintertime. Without them, the solitude of the High Cascades would be unbroken.

# CHAPTER III
## BIRDS

*Sweet is the breath of morn, her rising sweet,*
*With charm of earliest birds.*

*Paradise Lost, John Milton*
*(1608-1674)*

# EAGLE AT STEENS MOUNTAIN

One of the most unusual stories to come out of the Steens Mountains was told me recently by a friend.

A group of young riders had just climbed out of the Blitzen Gorge and stopped to rest their horses, when they noticed a bald eagle circling intently over one spot near the cliffs above them. Suddenly there was a movement in the grass below, and the eagle swooped down swiftly and struck at a little fawn that had been hidden.

The big bird hit the fawn savagely with his talons, but the fawn scrambled to its feet and began climbing over some boulders just below a ledge of rock.

Again the eagle struck and hit the fawn, knocking him into the rocks and down the steep hill. He rolled 20 or 30 feet among the boulders, but got gamely to his feet and began climbing toward the ledge again. The eagle dove repeatedly, but each time the fawn seemed to recover and start back up the hill in his frantic attempt to escape from his relentless enemy.

Finally, the fawn managed to get to a shelf of rock where a large deer had been standing motionless watching the struggle. This could have been the fawn's mother. He darted past the larger deer and disappeared into a cave just under the rims.

The riders knew the fawn was probably badly hurt and might die in the cave, so one of them left his horse and made his way cautiously on foot to a spot nearby. The large deer leaped away as he approached. He blocked the entrance to the cave and caught the fawn in his arms as it ran out.

Examination disclosed deep bloody gashes on the fawn's back and head, bad bruises and probable internal injuries.

The rider put the trembling little animal across his saddle and took him down to camp. Here he was fed warm milk and given as much care as possible. But two days later the fawn died.

This incident was rare experience. It is most unusual for anyone to witness a bald eagle stalking its prey in the wilds.

Bald eagles are huge birds, with wing spreads of six and a half to eight feet. They formerly occupied a major part of North America, stretching from Mexico to the Middle Hudson Bay. They have been reduced in two centuries to perhaps a hundredth or less of their former numbers, because they have been considered harmful predators, and because our regions of wild country and wild rivers are shrinking so fast.

Originally they were mainly fish-eating birds and consumed tons of dead and dying salmon and other fish. They have also helped to control the population of rabbits and rodents, and we should hate to see them eliminated entirely.

Those that are left are found in the most inaccessible wilderness areas of our country and are themselves a part of the beauty and interest of our national heritage.

# THE OWL HUNTS BY NIGHT

Just at dusk, the great horned owl flew from his perch in a big juniper tree out across the lake. A few minutes before, he had given his hunting call and received a reply from an aspen grove up in the hills. He was out to catch his evening meal. All day long he had perched in a dense tree, shielded from the bright light and hidden from the tormenting ways of the jays and crows. Now it was time to hunt. And he could take his pick from the geese and ducks roosting on the water with their heads tucked under their wings. A quick vicious strike, a few quacks and he had his meal.

The great horned owl's kills are not limited to ducks and geese. Rabbits, rats, small birds, grouse, quail and even an occasional farmer's chicken make up his fare. Many are the tales of the big owl attacking more than he can handle. Larger animals, such as house cats or small dogs, have been seized by an owl. Even a fur cap has been snatched from the head of a late evening traveler. One night, during an especially severe winter, something attacked our house cat. Upon hearing the cat squalling outside the kitchen door, I shined a flashlight on a big owl that had seized the gray furry animal, and then couldn't fly away with it. A lucky shot killed the bird without touching the cat.

Probably no more a voracious hunter is found in the bird family than the great horned owl. With inch-long talons he rips his prey, and his terrible beak finishes the kill. The killing may be very destructive when a farmer's poultry or game birds are the victims. At other times, when mice or other rodents are destroying the fields, the owl may be a boon to the farmer.

The owl's greatest enemy is the crow. Both jays and crows love to find a sleepy owl in a tree, and then relentlessly tease and torment him. A call that an owl has been found will bring all the crows within hearing distance. A great hubbub will ensue until the owl leaves for other territory. At night it is another story. It is the owl's turn to harass the crows.

# OSPREYS ARE IMPOSING SIGHTS

Every morning, just as the first rays of the sun touched our lake, he would visit us. Coming from the south over a thick wall of trees, he would drop on swift and silent wings. Our first warning that he had arrived was his piercing series of sharp cries. It was almost as though he was saying, "I'll kill, kill, kill!" This alone indicated his species. He was an osprey—a fish-eating hawk, not unlike a small eagle.

The osprey is one of our largest hawks. With a wing spread of four to six feet, he is indeed an imposing sight as he dives from 50 to 100 feet, feet first, into the water. He is the only hawk that dives for fish. On beating wings, he hovers for an instant over the water as he locates a fish near the surface. He plunges with a terrific splash, coming up with the fish in his claws. As he flies away, he first stops in mid-air to shake the water from his feathers, then turns the fish in his claws so it will be carried head first to eliminate air friction.

The osprey is widely found along our lakes and streams. The fact that he fishes by sight restricts him to clear water. Where man has polluted and discolored the stream, the osprey must move on. He is found from the far north to his wintering grounds in the south.

A few of us have been privileged to witness a bald eagle robbing a fish hawk of his catch. When the osprey has made a catch, the eagle dives at him with a scream, causing him to drop his fish. The fish is then caught by the eagle before it reaches the water.

Some of the most conspicuous nests found along our streams are those of the osprey. The nest will be perched high on a sharp pinnacle of rock or in the top of a dead tree. It will be a mass of sticks, sometimes several feet thick, with a soft lining of grass or bark. The eggs, numbering from two to four, are beautifully marked with brown. They are very large compared to the size of the bird.

On several occasions, while making river trips, we have climbed to an osprey's nest. The adult birds will scream and dive at us so closely that we feel the wind from their wings, but they do not actually attack. If young birds are found in the nest, they will be lying flat and very quiet—obedient children to their parents' warnings.

Fishermen should take note of the method used by the ospreys in catching their quarry. It is the most sporting of all. Whereas the fisherman uses hook and line, the hawk uses his "hands." Should not a fisherman of this caliber be unmolested and given free play along our streams? The very few fish that he would take would be more than compensated for by the thrill of seeing him make a catch.

# LET HAWKS AND OWLS ALONE

A fast-moving hawk swooped low over the trees. The hunter fired and a puff of feathers indicated that a direct hit was made. With a smug smile of satisfaction, the hunter continued on his way, content that he had saved his quota of game birds that day. All too often this happens along the coastal and mountain flyways of North America.

Hunters justify the kill in the belief that the hawk or owl is competing in their bird hunting. Some farmers shoot hawks or owls on sight. A hawk on top of a tall tree is an inviting target to any gunner.

Unless some real protection is forthcoming, the hawks and owls will soon follow the trail of the passenger pigeon or the whooping crane. Each year their ranks grow thinner. Their habitat is fast disappearing, and more and more people are encroaching on their wilderness territory.

In the past, attempts have been made to classify hawks and owls into beneficial or destructive groups. The Cooper's hawk, sharp shinned hawk and goshawks were supposed to be the bad actors of their species. All other hawks were considered beneficial to the farmers. Likewise, the great horned owl was condemned as being too destructive to wildlife, while the rest of the owl family was considered helpful. Now opinions are changing, and all the hawks and owls are considered of some use. Their predatory qualities are more than offset by their good deeds in controlling rodent population.

As nature produced a given species of bird or animal, nature also provided a check on this species in the form of predators. Most all fish, birds or animals can reproduce far beyond the carrying capacity of their habitat. Some must die every year so that others may carry on. Predators perform the job of weeding out the weak, the sick and the unadaptable, leaving a healthy stock to carry on. In this way, predators are necessary to all species. And the predator keeps a species in check with far less cruelty than starvation and disease.

Predators have a great tendency to collect where the prey is most abundant. If favorable conditions have built up a surplus population of rabbits or mice, predators move in to reduce the population to the normal carrying capacity. Note what happened in Klamath and Lake Counties when coyotes and bobcats were almost eliminated by poisoning. The rabbit and mouse population literally exploded; whole fields of grass and grain were destroyed in a short time. Then the owls and hawks moved in. In some fields I noted hundreds of owls catching mice. Hawks were perched everywhere getting their share. In a few months the mice were reduced to normal numbers.

This same condition could exist in the songbird population. Although we hate to see any songbird destroyed, it might become necessary in an over-populated area. Thus hawks and owls have been placed here for a purpose, and it is not up to man to destroy them. The next time you see a hawk or owl perched in the top of a tree, refrain from taking a shot at him. Sit down and watch him soar high in the sky or listen to his shrill warning scream and realize that he has a right to live, a place in nature's plan.

# THE HONKER MEANS FALL

No call of the wild is so indicative of the seasons as that of the Canadian honker as he goes south in the fall to warmer lands or north in the spring to his nesting grounds. This annual migration has always meant the coming of fall or spring. The call of the wild honker on his way north brings an uneasy feeling to man. He wants to join the migration and discover for himself the far places of the north.

In ever-changing "V" formations, the geese follow age-old routes of migration. The leaders of the flock continuously change places with the birds at the point of the "V," as they break a path through the wind currents. The "V" formation allows every bird to see ahead, yet get the benefit of the slip stream of his companion.

The nesting period is April and May. Four to seven white eggs are laid in a nest of reeds, sticks or other handy material, and they are covered with down. From the time the goslings hatch, they are good swimmers and divers. Their nesting grounds may be on most any waterway of North America, but the bulk of the geese go to the far north and to the Arctic watershed. Quite a number of birds nest in Oregon on the lakes or remote rivers.

The Owyhee and John Day Rivers are favorite nesting places. On our spring trips on these rivers, we see a great many pairs, some with their broods of downy yellow goslings and some still sitting on the nest. We have seen Canadian honkers nesting on rock ledges from six to thirty feet above the water, to protect their nests from predators.

When the young are old enough to take to the water, the parents either coax them out of the nest or push them out. The goslings tumble to the water, join their brood and start the never-ending search for food. When danger comes to them from the water, the young can dive and swim under water for many feet, coming to the surface for air and instantly diving again. On rare occasions, when the presence of a boat threatens them, they will climb out on the shore and hide in the thick brush.

Adult honkers have been known to attack a human when close to their nest. Usually the parents will try to decoy danger away from their young by simulating a broken wing. After the pursuer has been decoyed far enough, the old geese will rise and fly back to their young.

Sometimes when a Canadian honker is sneaking away from danger, he will sink into the water until only his head and the top of his back will be visible. How such a huge bird can make himself so inconspicuous is one of nature's little tricks of survival.

One day, while we were having lunch at the foot of a swift rapids, a little family group of geese appeared on their way upstream. To make the portage, they took to the land, where the mother goose led with the little goslings in a line behind. Bringing up the rear was the old gander. It would have taken a pretty brave predator to attack this group. The old geese can hit a terrific blow with their wings.

Honk, honk, honk, and everybody rushes outdoors to see the long "V" of birds headed for the north. We hope the day never comes when we no longer hear that thrilling sound.

# A SHREWD, BOLD BIRD

A light snow dusted the trees and ground when we awoke at our camp in the pine forest. Suddenly we heard a hoarse, raucous cry, followed by a dry rattling sound. Nearby perched a large black bird. To entice him closer, we threw some bread slices on the ground. He flew down almost immediately and tentatively sampled first the brown bread and then the white. Then, to our amazement, he placed two slices together sandwich fashion, took a firm hold on both with his strong beak and flew off to enjoy his feast.

This bird was the raven, one of the smartest of our common birds, and one which is widely distributed over North America. His glistening blue-black plumage immediately identifies him as the big cousin of the crow. From dull black to bluish green to iridescence, his colors change with the light. His large, heavy beak also distinguishes him from the crow. And his calls and noises are legion. He seems to imitate many birds, and, when these calls are exhausted, he croaks, rattles and clacks like dry bones in the wind.

He is credited with being shrewd, quick-witted, audacious, and even sinister. In past history, he has been held omnipotent and has played an important part in religious rituals. He has even had poetry written about him. Probably no other bird has played such a dominant part in North American history.

One of the good things about the raven is his habit of patrolling the highways to clean up the dead animals. On the other hand, he will just as willingly feed on the hunter's prize buck, if it has not been well protected. It is an amazing thing to watch the ravens gather at the scene of a kill. No sooner will a deer be killed, than a single raven will be noticed in the sky. By some means known only to the raven clan, the bird will give a signal and soon the sky is dotted with birds coming to the carcass.

A number of years ago we were on a boat trip on the John Day River. We noticed several young ravens on an old abandoned windmill tower. They were too young to fly, so we captured two of them and took them along as mascots on the trip. Their nest had been constructed of old beef rib bones for framework and lined with sticks and hair or wool from some dead animal.

The ravens proved to be good pets and ate anything we would offer them. When riding in the boat, they would look out through the cracks in their box and give their hoarse calls to any passing bird in the sky. They were later brought to Eugene and kept as pets for several months. After long flights around the area, they would return and scratch on the back door to be let in.

Ravens are found far north in Alaska and south in Mexico. Some do not migrate but winter in the frigid North. It is a puzzle what they find to eat. The birds along the coast feed on shell fish and find food in abundance, but a snow-covered landscape is another matter. Ravens are omnivorous and will eat insects, carrion, seeds, fruit and any garbage discarded by man. They are most fond of young birds and eggs, and this is where they do the most damage. They hunt tirelessly for nests to destroy, and only a very few birds are fierce enough to drive them away.

The raven seeks wild and inaccessible places to nest, perhaps on a ledge high in the cliffs. Any handy native material is used. After the nest has been lined with some soft material, from three to six light blue-green eggs splotched with brown or olive are deposited.

No other bird will risk raiding a raven's nest, so they are safe. Only man has made inroads on his numbers.

# BOLD MOUNTAIN SENTRY

A loud raucous call comes from the tree tops. At intervals it is repeated, first as a noise not unlike that of a common crow, then as the harsh scolding voice of a bird trying to drive an interloper away.

This is your introduction to the Clark's nutcracker of the High Cascades—sometimes known as the Clark's crow. He is a large bird, predominately light gray with white patches on black wings and tail. He cannot be confused with any other bird in the high mountains if the white patches are seen. He lives in conifer forests from an elevation of 4,000 feet to timberline. He is undoubtedly the noisiest bird in the woods, even surpassing the stellar jay. He is disliked by other birds for his loud voice and his nest robbing tendencies, and sometimes will be chased out of an area by a band of smaller birds.

Flying from the top of one tall snag to another, he lets all comers know that this is his territory. Even larger animals, such as deer and elk, heed his call of warning. In the fall, a smart old buck is alerted by the nutcracker's warning cry. Who is a better watchman than this keen-eyed bird perched high on the top of a dead tree?

The nutcracker combines some of the characteristics of the Lewis woodpecker and the jay. He eats insects as well as berries and alights on the ground in search of grubs or grasshoppers. He is not adverse to stealing tidbits from the camper's table or even invading his tent. His more stable food, that of seeds from pine or fir cones, must be removed from cones still hanging on the tree. The bird can hold the cone firmly with one strong foot, while the other clasps the limb and steadies him. The powerful bill works like a small crowbar to gouge out the seeds.

These birds nest in late February or March while there is still snow on the ground, and they are so quiet at this time that one might think that they have left the country. A warm nest is made of twigs and interlaced with strips of bark to form a deep bowl for the eggs. Two or three green spotted eggs are laid and must be closely incubated during the cold weather. The young birds are fed tiny seeds. At the time that other birds are nesting, the nutcrackers have their family raised and can spend a leisurely summer They do not migrate in the usual sense, but stray birds have been found in unusual places. They have been noted by climbers at the top of very high peaks during the late summer months.

When the great storms of late fall and winter hit the mountains, think of this hardy bird remaining in the severe climate, with the forests whipped by strong winds, snow and below freezing temperatures. This is his home, and here he will stay until the coming of another spring.

# WESTERN HARLEQUIN DUCK

A lonely vigil is being kept on a certain moss-covered rock in Bear Creek rapids. Since early last fall a little western harlequin duck has adopted this locality for his home. He was injured some time last summer and could not migrate when the rest of his family left for the south. Now he is waiting for their return.

The western harlequin is a small, brightly colored duck known to the foaming mountain streams of the Northwest. The male is gaudily striped with white paint on a chestnut background. Ten stripes on each side readily earns him the name of harlequin. The female is more somber, lacking the stripes, but with a round white spot near the ear.

Each spring these little ducks return to the McKenzie to nest and spend the summer; then, in very early fall, they leave on their migration. They are the first ducks to return, however. They nest near the water under a log or overhanging rock or tree root. The eggs, numbering six to ten, are cream or olive-buff colored. Their food, consisting of periwinkles, snails, and various forms of insect life, is readily available in the shallow water.

To quote from Vernon Bailey, "the harlequin duck is rare enough in the United States to excite keen interest, especially when found on its breeding grounds. A little flock of the richly barred and spotted beauties fishing in a foaming mountain stream, diving, bobbing on the rough surface, drifting or darting down over the rapids, and then gathering in a bunch below to fly back up stream for another descent, suggests a lot of school boys on a coasting party rather than a flock of birds engaged in the serious business of getting breakfast. They seem to enjoy the icy water and their power to dare and buffet its torrents."

Next spring, when you are fishing the McKenzie, watch for these little ducks skimming over the water on their way up stream or floating leisurely down the current, frequently ducking their heads under the water as though they were looking for something. They add their bit of beauty and interest to your day.

# THE THRUSH LOVES RAIN

There is no sound in the woods of the Northwest more thrilling or mysterious than the song of the varied thrush. He loves rain as a fish loves water, and as a gentle spring drizzle descends on forest and earth, from the top of a tall fir there will come his single drawn-out note of melancholy beauty.

The thrush is known by a variety of names. Perhaps you have known him as a swamp robin, Alaskan robin or winter robin. These birds spend their summers in the deep woods of the high mountains. In severe winters they may migrate as far south as the desert country, but in mild winters they remain near their summer territory, migrating lower only when big storms hit.

Living in the valley, one can always tell when a winter snowstorm has hit the high country. The varied thrush appear in large numbers, looking for bare ground. They are mainly ground feeders, and, with lightening-like thrusts of their bills, they meticulously turn over each leaf in search of hidden worms or insects. Some morning you may notice that the ground under your apple trees has been disturbed. A band of varied thrush has been there early in search of food.

In appearance the thrush is about the size of a robin, but with a distinctive blackish band across the chest and wings of tawny yellowish markings. The male will be more brightly colored than the female.

In late spring, they make a large, well-constructed and

elegant nest deep in the darkest forests. The nest is made of several layers of twigs, sticks and mosses, with the innermost lining of neatly woven dried grass and moss. Even though the outside layer of the nest may be wet, this inner section is always dry and soft. There are often two broods of young birds, with three eggs laid for each brood. Eggs are pale to light green, speckled with chocolate markings. Thrushes observe a division of territory, nests usually being built no closer than a half mile apart.

Besides the melodious single call which the thrush gives, there is also their loud chirp of alarm, and a long, drawn out "shee-ee" which they give when calling to one another at their feeding grounds.

# REDWINGS RETURN FROM SOUTH

There was great excitement in the pasture this morning. The redwinged blackbirds had arrived from the south. What a world of happiness and jubilation there was in their whistling, chirping, and song. Flying from tree to tree, alighting for only an instant, then swooping down to the ground, chattering all the time, their exuberance dispelled any thought of more winter.

For several months the birds had been wintering in the Sacramento Valley. In flocks of many thousands they had fed in the rice and grain fields by day then returned to the tulle swamps to roost, their weight bending the cattails to the earth.

Now in smaller flocks, they were returning to their summer homes in the north, where they would nest and rear their young. Upon arriving at their destination, they would stake out their territory for the brooding period. Each pair of birds would have a specific territory upon which to hunt for food and guard from other blackbirds. On the busy highways of the Willamette Valley, the redwings lay claim to certain section of road on which to catch their insects. A passing car will kill the flying insects, and the birds gather them up. Woe to any other blackbirds that try to trespass on this territory.

The redwing blackbird, with the brilliant red epaulets on his wings, is one of our most numerous birds, ranging from Southern California to Canada. The male redwing is the one that carries the color. The female is a dark brown with contrasting streaks of light brown. They are very numerous in the grain fields and earn their keep by destroying insects. It is said that each blackbird in an alfalfa crop is worth a dollar.

The eggs of the redwing are a beauty to behold. The delicately colored bluish-green is mottled with specks of brown, black or purple. Two, three or four eggs in a well-made nest are hatched in 14 days; in another two weeks the young are ready to leave the nest. During this time the adults jealously guard the nesting ground, chasing away all intruders. A furious "clack, clack" indicates their anger, and the male will fluff his brilliant red patches as much as to say, "this is the warning signal." They will so annoy and harass a hawk or crow that it is obliged to leave. I have even seen them chase an eagle.

The morning song of the redwing is one of the most beautiful of all bird melodies. Sometimes it sounds like tiny bells tinkling, other times it is the melodious "kon-ger-reee." This is the male's mating song. On some Eastern Oregon rivers it is most noticeable, as every foot of the river bank is claimed by some pair of birds.

With the coming of fall and migration time, the excitement starts again. The summer broods collect in great flocks and begin their training for the long flight south. Clouds of birds fly into a tree crowding each other off the limbs. They are mustering again for the trip south.

# RETURNING BIRDS

One of these early spring mornings, you will awaken to find the yard full of returning birds. Their short winter in the south is over and they have returned to their home territory and nesting grounds.

What great excitement there is. Birds are flying everywhere. Suddenly they all light in the yard and begin searching for worms. Then just as suddenly they take off at a danger signal. Chirping, twittering and scolding, they are like a group of children on a school picnic. They are happy to be back, and now comes the job of finding suitable nesting areas and defending these premises from all comers.

The large family of woodpeckers will probably be the noisiest of the lot. Tapping on a dry tree trunk, they will be sending out their messages to others of their kind. Then, in not so rhythmical patterns, they will be boring into the hard dry wood for a grub or beetle. Every so often they will send out the sharp calls so peculiar to the woodpecker family, and the loudest noise of all will be the clarion call of the big pileated woodpecker. His call is music to the woods. The Indians called him the raincrow and maintained that he only called before a storm.

The most numerous of the returning birds will be the red-breasted robins and varied thrush. Many of them have not migrated at all, but just dropped lower in the valley as the snow covered the high country. With the melting of snow, the varied thrush will be the first to push back into the dense timber of the mountains. They like the solitude and protection of the heavy forest.

Among the early arrivals will be the black birds or grackles. They will be feeding with the robins, varied thrushes, red-shafted flickers, and juncos. Notice their little mincing steps. The other birds will be hopping over the ground.

Many of the smaller birds, like the chickadees, sparrows and kinglets, will not be so noticeable. However, you can hear them in the trees, twittering and chirping and joining in the excitement. The plaintive call of the white-breasted nuthatch will be heard in the distance.

Following these birds will be the swift hawks, taking their toll whenever they are hungry.

With the melting of snow and coming of warmer weather, the birds will spread out all through the valleys and mountains. It is nesting time again.

# SANDHILL CRANES

The nostalgic calls of the sandhill cranes came to us from the valley as we watched the scene from our vantage point on Jack Mountain, which rises behind French Glen and overlooks the Malheur Game Refuge. The intriguing valley was full of sights and sounds: fields of harvested grain and grazing cattle, willow thickets sheltering pheasants and quail, high escarpments of rock which seemed to divide the valley like natural fences, the little Blitzen River winding its way north, and a medley of wild bird calls in the air.

Among the many other birds which this refuge shelters, there are 75-100 breeding pairs of greater sandhill cranes, as well as an additional 100 non-breeders which have been on the refuge during the past few years. These interesting birds, which stand three to four feet tall, and may have a wing spread of better than six feet, are native to Eastern Oregon. They were common residents of Harney, Lake and Klamath counties when the white men arrived.

During spring and fall migrations, the refuge population of sandhill cranes may increase to around 2,000 birds, which are feeding and resting between flights. Peak population generally occurs during the last half of March or the first of April and again in the fall during the first half of October. Evidence collected by biologists indicates that many of the cranes on the Malheur refuge winter in the Central Valley of California.

In the spring, cranes indulge in curious antics of courtship. The male bows with outstretched wings and nearly touches his beak to the ground. The females return the bow with equal grace. Then the birds take part in a dance which consists of swaying, leaping, high kicks and capers. As many as twenty couples may be going through these movements at the same time. As the birds are extremely shy and secretive, it is a rare privilege to see this courtship dance.

The nest of the cranes may be a small haystack of grasses placed on a slight rise so that the female can be alert to the approach of an intruder. Two eggs are laid, so beautifully colored like the surroundings that they are practically invisible to the casual observer.

Let us hope the time never comes when we cannot hear, in some far northern meadow, the lonely bugling calls of the sandhill cranes.

# SONG SPARROWS ARE WELCOME

A flash of brown streaks past the window and disappears in the holly tree. Quickly we identify the caller as a song sparrow. Our winter has been enlivened by the presence of several pairs of these cheerful little birds who have been the most faithful visitors to the feed board.

One pair of the mottled brown birds have made their headquarters in a pile of brush near the creek. Several times a day they wing their way across the clearing. The same pattern of travel is followed each time.

Flying close to the ground with an uneven, erratic flight, they are always ready to dart into hiding at the approach of an enemy.

Alighting in the lower branches of the holly, they work their way upward from limb to limb till they reach the board which holds wild bird seed, crumbs and suet. When they finish, they fly to an apple tree and reward us with their song.

This joyous song is like the tinkling of tiny bells and resembles that of the house wren. Any little upward change in temperature will cause the song sparrow to fly up on a bush and rehearse his cheerful melody.

Another pair of song sparrows lives around the woodshed. They sometimes fly into the feed barrels or invade the workshop in search of grain or tidbits of food. A third pair make its home farther up the creek. Each pair stays in its own territory, apparently an agreement understood by sparrows, but not binding on other birds.

Song sparrows like being near people and can become quite tame. They love water and can sometimes be seen splashing in a shallow pool. Young birds are a choice morsel for almost anything that preys—cats, skunks, weasels, hawks, crows, jays and garter snakes. For this reason, sparrows raise three or four broods a season.

Nests are a substantial structure of twigs, weed stems or moss, placed low in clumps of brush or in old stumps. Three or four eggs will be laid for each incubation. This requires only twelve days, and, in another twelve, the young birds are able to fly. If they did not have so many enemies, the earth would soon be overrun with song sparrows.

There are several varieties of song sparrows, each taking on the characteristics of the area which he frequents. But all have the general brown-streaked appearance, underparts grayish white with darker gray markings. They are non-migratory and feed mainly on weed seeds.

It is late afternoon, and soon the song sparrows will be making their last trip to the feed board. When another day dawns, their happy little songs will be heard throughout the woods.

# THE TANAGER, SHY AND COLORFUL

A flash of scarlet drew our attention to the holly tree, and a brilliantly colored bird about the size of a song sparrow began devouring some of last year's berries. Our visitor was the western tanager, one of the four species of tanagers that reach the United States from their home in the tropics.

The male western tanager, sometimes called the crimson-headed or Louisiana tanager, has a beautiful red head and throat, back, wings and black tail, with wings tipped by white or yellow. The rest of the bird, including the short notched bill, is a rich yellow. The female resembles the male in size, but shows no red coloring and has a dull olive back, yellow breast and some white on the wing bars.

Tanagers are shy birds, probably feeling conspicuous in their bright colors. They remain in thick trees and brush and are constantly on the move when they are out in the open.

Only the mature males have the vivid coloring, and this fades to a more protective drabness before the birds make their migratory flight to their winter homes in South America.

The spring migration of male western tanagers, which may precede the arrival of the females by several days, is a beautiful sight. On their way north, they may stop to feed on fruit and berries and may make great inroads on a berry patch. Their diet consists of fruit and insects, but not seeds.

After the male tanager has selected his mate, she proceeds

with the nest building. He does not help with this work, nor to any great extent with the rearing of the young.

The mother bird makes a substantial but rather roughly constructed nest of twigs, small roots and weed stems, and lines it with horse or cow hair. It is a shallow saucer-like nest near the tip of a pine or fir branch. Eggs are light bluish-green spotted with dark olive.

Recently, we found a year-old nest in the Metolius area which had a modern note. Interwoven with the horsehair were narrow strands of aluminum foil which is sometimes dropped from planes in weather observations. This bird had discovered the advantages of modern insulation!

The spring song of the western tanager somewhat resembles that of the robin, but it is shorter and uttered at intervals instead of being a continuous melody. It is sometimes mistaken for that of the robin.

It is a great sight to see tanagers catching insects over the river. They perch on limbs near the water, and, as the hatch of flies comes out, they plunge and swoop low catching several to carry home to the nest of hungry babies. They are able to catch a number of insects, holding them securely in their mouths till they are fairly bristling with feelers, before returning to the nest.

In times of insect infestation, tanagers are known to collect great numbers. For this reason they are not only beautiful birds, but also beneficial.

# OREGON JUNCO

We were walking along a little path in the heavy forest when suddenly a small bird darted out like a flash, almost under our feet. It seemed to have come from the ground itself, and it shot away a short distance as though it wished to be pursued.

This was an Oregon junco, and we were near its nest. It had stayed on the nest till the last possible moment, then darted away to lure us from the area. Tucked in a little crevice under a clump of grass, we found a tiny nest of twigs, grass stems, and soft materials. Three pale eggs, camouflaged with brownish streaks and flecks, were laid in the neat hiding place.

This nesting location is peculiar to the junco. He always seems to place his nest on or near the ground, and it is so cleverly hidden that very close scrutiny is necessary even when one sees the bird emerge from its home. The junco prefers a dirt bank overhanging a path or road, as this location provides shade and some security from snakes and other enemies. He needs the coolness which is provided by overhanging ferns or leaves.

The junco is one of our most common American birds. There are several species, and they can be found from the forests of the far north to the warm desert country of the south, and from sea level to the high mountains. The nesting periods will begin much earlier in lower elevations, but extend almost into fall in high country. It is thought that the same pair of birds may raise one brood early at low elevation and another at

6,000 to 8,000 feet in July or August.

The Oregon junco can be distinguished by its sparrow-like size, its glossy black head with white breast and white lateral tail feathers. These white tail feathers are sometimes used as signal flags when a flock of juncos suddenly decides to fly away. They often stay around all winter in our locality, not minding the cold, but perhaps migrating to lower elevations during big storms.

The junco's song is a sweet, tinkling trill, but he can also make small hissing sounds which may repulse enemies during the breeding season.

One year we were camped at about 7,000 feet elevation in the Three Sisters Wilderness Area when a terrific hail and thunderstorm occurred. It lasted about an hour, and hail stones the size of large marbles pelted down so thickly that they rolled into depressions like so many balls. The impact of the stones were so severe that many small birds were killed.

After the storm was over we went out to survey the damage. We found many dead juncos, as well as their ruined nests, all over the area.

# UNSOCIAL FISHERMAN

A lonely kingfisher winged his erratic way up the stream. This was his domain—his territory to fish and to guard from other fish-eating birds. His unsocial attitude allowed only members of his own family to fish in his chosen waters.

Every so often he would stop at one of his established perches. These vantage points afforded him a watching place for small fish in the shallow water below. From this perch, he would suddenly drop to the surface of the water with a great splash. Usually he came up with a small fish clasped in his long spear-like beak.

Unlike some of the other fish-eating birds who catch fish in their claws, the kingfisher possesses the accuracy to grab a fish in his beak. The unusual characteristic of this beak is that it has barbs to help him hold a slippery fish. Bringing it back up to his perch, he will hit it a few times against a branch, then swallow it head first.

The belted kingfisher is one of our most common fish-eating birds of lakes and streams. The belt of slate blue to brown across his breast gives him his name. He is about the size of a red-shafted flicker and has tiny feet placed far back under his torpedo-shaped body. These small feet are only for perching on a branch—the rest of the time they are folded up in his feathers. His entire shape is for diving

He builds his nest in a hole several feet back in a sand or earth bank. Each year the nesting pair digs a new hole. At the end of the hole a cavity is made, and very little material is used to make it soft. Perhaps a few leaves or small sticks. The eggs are pure white, and the young will number from four to seven. They are probably the ugliest of all bird youngsters. Picture the long beaked scraggly birds perched on a branch, awaiting the return of a parent bringing a dainty morsel of fish, frog or insect.

His shrill, rattling warning cry comes as a surprise to an interloper. The cry is not unlike rattling small balls in a wooden box. If necessary, the kingfisher is able to back up his warning with veritable dive bombing. His sharp bill can act as a spear.

It is said that a kingfisher eats his weight each day in fish. This could be devastating to a trout stream, if the food were all small trout. But he varies his diet with many trash fish, an occasional frog or salamander, and sometimes large insects.

# VALUABLE FOREST FLICKERS

A clear, repetitious, insistent bird call can be heard on sunny spring mornings in the McKenzie Valley. If you are keen of eye, you may see a red-shafted flicker clinging to the topmost part of an old dead snag. His call is varied with a loud staccato tapping, a coded message sent out to others of his kind. Perhaps he says, "spring is here—the day is clear."

The flicker, sometimes called the yellow hammer, high holder, or pigeon woodpecker, is just back from his winter in the south. Sometimes you may notice one bird appearing much larger than the others in a band of robins and varied thrush feeding in a yard or pasture. The larger bird may be the flicker, as these birds all feed together in friendly fashion.

Flickers are members of the woodpecker family and have many characteristics of this group of birds, using dead trees, stumps and snags, both for nesting and hunting food. The red-shafted flicker is the only one that I have noticed that also feeds on the ground. He is a beautifully marked bird. The flame color of his under wing surfaces are clearly seen in flight. He is brown, finely barred with black on his back, with underparts lighter, heavily barred and spotted with black. His head is marked with the same brilliant red that marks his shafts.

The long, prehensile, claw-like feet of the flicker allow him to cling to the side of a snag like a high climber, while he bores into the bark for grubs and insects. He has a long bracing claw below which gives him a better grip; the shafts in his stiff tail jut into the bark, almost giving him the appearance of having a shelf to perch on. His tongue is long and barbed and can be projected several inches beyond his beak to search out insects in deep crevices.

Snags are also the nesting places of these birds. On several occasions, when I have been hiking through the woods, I have noted a perfectly round hole in a dead tree or snag. Suspecting that it might be a flicker's home, I have tapped the trunk sharply. Almost immediately a head has popped out to investigate. The hole will be fairly deep and slant downward. The nest, usually lined only with wood chips, is snug and well protected against both weather and predators. Four to six white eggs are laid in late spring.

Flickers are very valuable birds in our forests. They keep the insects which destroy young timber well under control. For this reason, the good tree farm manager leaves a few snags in his forest to provide nesting places. One can imagine a forest so well kept, so cleared out of snags and dead trees, that the woodpecker families could find no nesting places or food. In a few years, these forests could be completely taken over by beetles and other pests.

The harmonious adjustment of birds and insects is all a part of the delicate balance so important to nature's overall plan.

# MASTER FISHERMAN

An old mother fish duck clucked softly to her brood, and they immediately gathered around her. Without a ripple on the water, they sneaked back into the willows. A boat was coming down the river and danger was near. After the fishermen had passed, the mother duck gave another call and the young joined her out in the stream. It was time to fish. Without an apparent signal, the young ducks all lined up for a foray in the swift current. Alternately swimming and diving, they combed the bottom for fish. Here and there a duck came up with a wriggling trout in his mouth. Sometimes the catch was a bullhead or young salmon. Whatever came into their moving net was taken.

The American merganser is one of the numerous predatory ducks found on all of our fishing streams and lakes. Protected by migratory waterfowl laws, it is infrequently shot by hunters, as it is not good to eat. Therefore, it is increasing beyond good biological controls.

Three species of fish-eating ducks are found on our streams: the American merganser, the redbreasted and the hooded. The latter is a beautiful duck with the male carrying a striking black and white crest. They are rarely found and are rigidly protected.

It is a large duck, almost the size of a mallard. It has a brown top knot that can be erected at will, and at a distance will be mistaken for a canvas back because of the gray patches. The male in mating plumage is a beautiful black and white bird. Nesting along all of our fish-producing streams and lakes, the mergansers hatch from six to fifteen young. Only the mother duck cares for the young ones. At first they have a diet high in aquatic insects, but in a short time, the young ducks are taught to catch fish. With their long slender bills lined with sharp teeth, they can easily hold a squirming trout. Even fish hiding under a rock can be reached with the long beak.

For the most part, a fish duck will nest along the border of a lake or river not far from the water's edge, but on two occasions I have seen mergansers nesting in the top of a high snag. It is interesting to speculate how they get the young to the water.

An adult merganser can take 50 small fry in a single day. He can actually consume trout up to eight inches or more. Almost always, when a duck is examined, one will find evidence of several trout or salmon. The gizzard will be packed with small bones of the digested fish.

# FEATHERED WEATHERMAN

The stillness of a quiet evening is suddenly shattered by a loud clarion call. It is the pileated woodpecker, or "rain crow" as the Indians call him, giving his forecast for rain. He was the Indians' weatherman and they claimed that he was almost infallible in his predictions.

The pileated is the largest of the western woodpeckers, and he ranges over many wooded sections of the Northwest. In some areas he is also known as the black woodcock. Similar in size to the crow and with his general plumage sooty black, he has some white on his throat and the lining of his wings. But his distinguishing feature is his scarlet crest, not only because of its brilliant color, but because it counterbalances the bill and gives the head its hammerlike appearance.

This crest was much sought after by the Indians of our coast and figured prominently as a personal decoration in their medicine dances.

The bill of the pileated is most unusual. Made apparently of horn, just as other birds', it seems to have some of the characteristics of steel. The bird uses it recklessly both as ax and crowbar, as it hews its way through the bark of our largest dead firs in its efforts to get the grubs between bark and wood. There is no mistaking the bark piles which surround the base of certain old snags. A pileated woodpecker has been working there.

An interesting fact is that the pileated does not always make round holes as do other woodpeckers—his often have square corners.

Possibly the most interesting feature of all is the woodpecker's tongue, which is able to protrude suddenly to a distance of four or five inches beyond the tip of its beak. With this long barbed tongue, he can reach in a very small hole and extract an insect. This is a great help to the bird in tracking down buried food.

The pileated woodpecker is particularly interested in decayed fallen logs. A pair of these birds will gradually tear a rotted log to pieces in search of grubs and wood-boring ants.

This bird chisels out its nesting hole at varying heights in dead timber, whether it be fir, pine or incense cedar. The nest usually holds three to five eggs, pure china white in color. An egg is deposited daily and incubation lasts about eighteen days. Both male and female assist in the incubation, as well as in caring for the young. Like all woodpeckers, the pileated are devoted parents, and the young follow them for some weeks after leaving the nest.

Once more the pileated woodpecker's call rings out through the dense green forest. "Rain before morning," he says. "Take care, take care." At close range it is full, melodious and clear—one of the most untamed sounds in the forest.

# HUMMER'S FLIGHT

A bright spot of color darts past the windows, hovers a moment near some blossoms, then as swiftly disappears, leaving a buzzing sound in the air. This is the flight of the hummingbird, the smallest and one of the most brilliantly colored members of the bird family.

There are a number of species, but the one we see most commonly in the Cascades is called the rufous hummingbird. He comes back to the valleys in quite early spring. As soon as the high alpine meadows are free of snow and dotted with wildflowers, this bright flyer is found everywhere. His presence adds interest and beauty to the mountain areas. We have put out sugar water in small feeders and attracted dozens of the birds to our camps. But we have never been successful in finding many of the nests, which are very tiny. Often they are hidden in the crotch of a limb and camouflaged with bits of lichen attached by spider webs.

The hummingbird has the most varied flight of any bird. The wings are attached to the shoulders by joints that permit a rotary motion, and the speed of the wing beats is so rapid that the human eye cannot follow it. This permits the bird to hover motionless, to fly backwards, or to dash ahead at an incredible speed. Their endurance, too, is known to be very great. Hummingbirds are said to migrate long distances non-stop over large bodies of water.

The feeding habits of these birds are similar in all of the species. They feed upon nectar, tiny insects and spiders, and seem to prefer red flowers. For this reason they love the brilliant blooms of the Indian paintbrush when it comes out in Linton Valley. The tongue of the hummingbird is very long and is a tiny hollow tube through which the nectar is drawn. The tip of the tongue is a little brush which makes the taking of insects much easier.

The female hummer is less brightly colored than the male, as is the case with most birds. She lays two tiny white eggs, maybe only a quarter of an inch long. The male does not help with the rearing of the young, but he attacks ferociously any other birds which come near his territory during this period. Their buzzing, whirlwind attack will often chase away birds much larger than themselves. They defend their winter feeding grounds in the same way.

The mother bird feeds her young by regurgitation and thrusts her long bill down the throat of the young in a seemingly reckless manner. However, the young seem to survive this rough treatment. Although they may stay in the nest as long as three weeks after birth, when they leave they are capable immediately of the fast flight of adult birds.

We are looking forward to investigating further the haunts of the hummingbirds in the high country. We know of a mountain hemlock thicket near the foot of the Three Sisters which literally buzzes with dozens of brightly colored hummers. At our approach, they will come out like an army on the attack, darting at our heads and almost trying to put out eyes in their fierce determination to protect their homes. In this thicket, we may sometime find their secret nesting place.

# JOYOUS WINTER WREN

Suddenly you see a fleeting glimpse of motion. You look at the spot, but it is gone. There it is again—the tiny flash of a wing, then a tiny bird appears. He comes up very close, apparently unafraid.

It is the winter wren—one of the smallest birds of our coniferous forests. Found throughout Oregon and, in fact, prevalent throughout the Northwest from Alaska to California, the winter wren is one of the most joyous birds of the deep woods.

Even before he appears, you might hear his tiny twittering voice. His notes are so high that only the best of ears will detect it. You imagine that you hear a little voice in the distance and, suddenly, he is almost beside you. He may be scolding you away from his territory or he may be welcoming you to share his bit of woods. His first inquiring notes will be a "chick, chick, chick;" later it may be the twittering and trilling of a real song. As it rings through the woods it expresses a quality of freedom and happiness.

He is a small, dark brown bird with a short tail and almost round body. But on his brown suit you will note a barred and speckled variation. His typical wren tail will give him away instantly.

The nest of the winter wren may be any nook or cranny in a bank, among rocks or in the crevices of roots. It will be well hidden and only visible to the well-trained eye. As one goes through the woods, a flash of color will give his nest location away. The nest itself is mostly a collection of moss, with some fine hair interwoven, or bits of fur or deer hair. In this well camouflaged nest will be laid three to five almost white eggs, speckled in brown. When the little birds hatch, they are probably the most trusting of all young birds. Sometimes they will be lined up on a log or limb, and, if one approaches very carefully, one can perhaps pick a youngster up.

The winter wren is the first to come to a bird call. Seat yourself in the dense woods on a log or at the base of a tree and remain motionless while giving a few twists of the call. Immediately, the dwellers of that territory will come to see who the intruder might be. As he inspects you, each little note will be accompanied by a bow or dip.

In the winter the wrens have a habit of gathering in fairly large groups for spending the night. A hole under an overhanging bank or hollow log might be their roost. A friend of mine once counted thirty-five wrens coming out of an old rolled up deer hide under his house. Night after night they would rendezvous there.

The next time you are in the woods, take time to visit with this friendly little bird. In an almost deserted woods, he will bring you cheer and company.

# THE CHUKAR IS A FINE IMPORT

Daylight was just breaking over the John Day Canyon, when the quiet was broken by a series of loud cackling calls coming from a high rim. It resembled the guinea hen, but this time it was the mating call of a male chukar.

Chukars are not native to North America. Years ago, several hundred of these birds were released in the central and eastern parts of Oregon. As their home habitat was the open grasslands and rimrock country of India, they readily took to the Eastern Oregon desert. Now they are found in great numbers and are rapidly becoming one of our best sporting birds.

Chukars are about the size of a small hen pheasant with an overall gray color barred with a rich rusty brown. The red legs and beak are their most distinguishing characteristics. At a distance, one might mistake them for mountain quail, but they are at least twice as large.

Nesting on the ground among clumps of sage or in tall grass, they bring out a large brood. In the early fall, after the young are grown, the chukars join other broods, making very large coveys. I have seen as many as two hundred birds in a band.

They love the high rimrock where, at the approach of an enemy, they can start climbing the rugged escarpment for refuge. This habit alone makes them difficult to hunt and ensures that they will not soon be killed off. With their long legs, they are great runners and will not fly unless hotly pursued.

Their flight is not unlike that of the quail, but they will not fly far. Lighting in the sage or on the rocks, they will hide for a short time then begin calling to get the flock together again. This characteristic gives the hunter an opportunity to flush them and get some good shooting.

One of the favorite tricks of an experienced hunter is to go into an area and make some loud startling noise such as sounding a predator call. This will immediately bring a warning call from any nearby covey, giving their location away.

Another feature that makes them a good sporting bird is that they are not dependent on farm or crop land for suitable living conditions. The cheat grass of the barren open grasslands of Eastern Oregon is one of their favorite foods. They may be found as far as 50 miles from the nearest ranch. With the vast amount of suitable habitat in Oregon, chukars promise to be one of our finest game birds.

# OUR QUAIL

The quail were collecting in the dense junipers as night approached, and their clear musical calls seemed to say, "Come right here, come right here." Soon the trees were full of birds talking softly and fluttering and changing places. In the dark, they would be quite safe from many of their enemies, with the exception of an owl who can spot a bird silhouetted against a juniper limb.

We were camped in a little grove at the mouth of a shallow canyon in Eastern Oregon. A rocky stream bed ran among the berry-laden trees, and beyond us lay the boundaries of the Malheur Game Refuge where we had seen ducks, deer, pheasants and chukar. The air was filled with the nostalgic cries of sandhill cranes and the lonely searching calls of migrating geese. Quail were all around us.

Quail are friendly, gregarious birds, and you may find them in coveys or bands which may number from a dozen to several hundred. A single bird will be the sentinel who watches for danger.

Whenever they are feeding or resting, this lookout will be stationed in a bush or on a rock nearby. Quail have many enemies including coyotes, bobcats, hawks, skunks and housecats. They are one of the fastest of upland game birds both in flight and on the ground.

One may hear the cheery little calls of mountain quail in many places in the foothills and higher valleys. Native to our area, they are a beautifully marked gray and brown bird about the size of a crow, with both male and female distinguished by a long straight head plume and a chestnut colored throat.

Summers are spent at higher elevations where the young are raised. But when the berries have been gleaned from the mountain berry patches, the birds begin a migration on foot to the lower valleys. They may winter near fields or barns where food is available. The call of the mountain quail is the true voice of the hills and high valleys.

California or valley quail are found in our lower valleys and desert country, where they have been introduced. They are smaller than their cousins of the mountains, and only the males have a short black head plume curving forward from the crown. Grayish in color, the males also have a black and white face and throat pattern.

The bobwhite is found in some areas in our state and widely in the east. He is browner in color and smaller in size. Because of his cheerful song, which really sounds like "bob white, bob-bob white", he has been placed on the protected "songbird" list in some northern states.

All species of quail make a grass lined nest on the ground in thick brush and brood a sizeable number of eggs (ten to twenty in a clutch). Mountain quail eggs are pale reddish, California eggs are buff and spotted, and bobwhite eggs a pure white.

When hatched they are very tiny, but, like many wild birds, they can almost run from the egg, and are adept at hiding under leaves or rocks. When the young are grown, the families join with other groups to form coveys of 50 or more.

I have often given the whistling call of the mountain quail and have brought the curious little birds within a few feet of where I was hidden. California quail can also be attracted by an imitation of their call.

Just at dawn in the desert country, one can hear the stir and flutter of wakening quail. After a visit to a spring or stream, the foraging begins. They feed on seeds, buds and berries in copious quantities. Thousands of seeds can be found in the maw of one bird. Quail are a great help to farmers, as they consume many weed seeds.

The heat of the day is spent in the shade of trees or brush, but, with the lengthening shadows of afternoon, the covey begins its search for food. Evening finds them again in the safety of the junipers.

# MOTHER BLUE GROUSE

The blue grouse moved cautiously as the first chicks in her clutch of twelve mottled eggs began to hatch. Her nest was well hidden under a hazel bush in a tangle of ferns. The long dried stems of last year's growth helped to camouflage her secret hiding place. She blended so perfectly with her surroundings that one could pass within a few feet and never see her. This was important, as there is hardly a predator in the woods that is not the enemy of the grouse.

Three days later all of the downy chicks were hatched. The grouse made her first venture forth in search of food, leaving her nest and calling urgently for the chicks to follow. She made her way to a small stream where she had her first drink in several days; then began scratching among the dead leaves to turn up insects. The chicks were fast but unbelievably tiny. They soon learned their first lessons in survival.

One morning a weasel, who was just losing his last winter's coat of white and was now a brownish cream color, heard the grouse clucking to her brood. Sly and quick, he crept upon the scene. The grouse was suddenly aware of danger and gave the signal for the chicks to hide under leaves or roots and freeze there. All hid except one chick, who was too slow and was grabbed by the weasel. The mother grouse flew into the woods to lure the predator away and came back later to collect her brood.

Just at dusk a few days later, when she was seeking a safe place for the night, a great horned owl snatched a chick in his claws and flew away in the darkness. The despairing cries of the young grouse were heard by all, but there was no help for him.

The next morning the grouse led her brood out into a sunny meadow to get grasshoppers. A hunting coyote hit the scent in the damp grass, and, in spite of a quick warning from mother grouse, the last chick in line was snapped up. Once more the old bird feigned a broken wing and flapped ahead of the coyote across the meadow. When she was far enough away, she flew up into a tree. The coyote went back where he had first found the brood, but was not successful in finding any of the chicks. They remained perfectly motionless and hidden until the old one came back to get them.

The young grouse were growing fast, and soon the mother was teaching them to fly. As soon as they could fly well, they would be much safer from prowling enemies on the ground. One day, as they were feeding in the woods, a hungry bobcat happened along. They all took to the air, but the bobcat was very fast and grabbed one out of mid-air. The rest reached safety in the limbs of a chinquapin, and the mother grouse took stock of the number she had left.

Danger was everywhere. One time a Cooper's hawk, or blue diver as they are sometimes called, suddenly appeared as the birds drank from a little pool. Swift and silent, he swooped and made off with another of the chicks before the band could get in the trees. There were only seven young left, but they were getting stronger and wiser all the time.

This band survived the summer and by fall were almost fully grown. Seven young birds had survived to renew nature's cycle.

# SHY FOREST DRUMMER

One of the most enchanting sounds in our woods is the distant drumming of the ruffed grouse. Often beginning in late February and lasting well into May, this sound is the mating song of the male grouse. But it may occur in the fall or at other times of the year, as it is also a song of exuberance. The ruffed grouse drums as other birds sing—just to express his joy of living.

Every cock has his log which he has chosen for his private drumming ground, and he is seldom heard elsewhere. The female may be located nearby in some deep thicket. The drumming call itself is deceiving; sounding far off in the distance, it may be only a hundred feet away. This call, which comes as a muffled, repetitious sound, rather resembles the noise made by the starting of a small motor and can carry long distances in the woods.

The drumming sound is not made by the bird drumming its wings on a log as some people believe, but by the bird beating its wings swiftly toward its breast. The wingbeat commences slowly, but increases its tempo and ends in a rapid whirr.

While the female watches in admiration, let us describe this shy inhabitant of our northwestern woods. His plumage is a warm brown and buff with touches of white. The neck has a "ruff" of glossy black. This ruff, or collar of feathers, is the most distinctive thing about the ruffed grouse plumage.

When the male is strutting, this ruff of inky black feathers stands out stiffly from the bird's throat and adds greatly to the beauty of his appearance. The grouse is about the size of a large hawk and blends in perfectly with his surroundings. The female is similar to the male, but her colors are muted and the neck ruff much reduced in size.

The grouse's nest may be only a slight depression, scantily lined with twigs and dried leaves, at the base of a tree or bush clump in low woods. There can be from eight to fourteen eggs of creamy white, faintly flecked with pink or buff, to a clutch.

The female grouse, who does most of the work of hatching and raising the young, is very secretive about her nest. She often flutters a few leaves over the eggs when leaving in order to camouflage the nest's location.

We have often come across a mother grouse and her brood along trails or wooded roads. The young are exquisitely tiny and unbelievably fast in hiding themselves. Often the mother grouse may charge right in the face of an intruder and simulate a broken wing to decoy the enemy away. This will give her brood a chance to disappear under leaves or in crevices of rocks. After the danger is over, the mother calls the brood back together again with a quiet little clucking call.

One of the earliest nature lessons was learned by a young lad who is now a grown-up conservationist. This boy used to take long walks near his home on the McKenzie, usually taking his .22 rifle along. Every spring he heard the drumming of grouse in a certain locality. Time after time he crept cautiously to an opening in the woods, hoping to catch the grouse at work on his log. But always the grouse anticipated him, and the log was never occupied.

One day he planned a circuitous route, and, circling a good distance, he approached behind the spot where the drumming was going on. He took a lot of time and was very quiet. He finally arrived at his planned spot and carefully parted the brush in front of him. Much to his joy he saw the grouse directly ahead, and not thirty feet away! He felt elated. Finally he had outwitted the wily old grouse, who was now at his mercy.

Just as he raised his gun to sight, the grouse, unaware of danger, stretched himself to his full height, and bringing his wings forward, began his drumming. There was wild freedom and joy in the sound. The boy sat quietly. Again and again the grouse gave his call while the boy watched and listened. The female appeared at last and they went off together, undisturbed by the boy. The beauty of the experience was never forgotten.

# CHAPTER IV

# WILDLIFE
# (AND A FEW WILD PERSONS)

*God could cause us considerable embarrassment by revealing all the secrets of nature to us: we should not know what to do for sheer apathy and boredom.*

Goethe (early 19th century)

## GRAY WOLF ONCE A LEGEND

A long drawn-out howl echoed up and down the valleys of South Fork. The moon was just coming up, and a dim light filtered down through the deep forest. The only other sound was the deep, muffled roar of the South Fork stream. Again the call sounded, and this time it was preceded by two or three hoarse barks, followed by a long howl. It was the voice of the gray timber wolf, and probably one of the last of his kind to be heard in the McKenzie country.

The time was the winter of 1935 before a road was built up the South Fork. I was hunting up this valley, in the snow, for cats and cougars. Late one afternoon, the dogs took a track and ran across the valley, stopping near the junction of the South Fork with Roaring River. As it was getting near sundown, I hurriedly followed the dogs and found them treeing a bobcat.

Shooting and skinning the cat took only a few minutes, and I headed back to camp at the old Dompier cabin. As I crossed Roaring River on a small log, one of the hounds refused to walk the log and sat down in the snow and began to howl. Thinking it would follow as soon as I had disappeared, I kept on traveling. Soon the other two hounds bristled up and looked back on the trail, but no dog appeared. The hounds seemed nervous and upset.

That night the dog did not come to camp, so I went back to the log crossing. There on the other bank, I found the remains of the hound. By the tracks in the snow, I knew the story. Two big wolves had heard it howling and had come down the ridge to make their kill.

In the early days of the McKenzie Valley, I had quite a few experiences with wolves. One time a companion and I skied into Clear Lake in mid-winter. The snow was four or five feet deep, and, as night overtook us before reaching the lake, we camped not far from the outlet. While we were making camp we heard the howl of a wolf at the upper end of the lake. It was soon followed by an answer on a high ridge across the valley; then a third wolf howled right back of camp. To say that it makes your hair stand on end is not far from the truth. Anyone who has heard wolves howl will verify that one can feel a prickly feeling at the back of his neck.

After spending a restless night around the fire, we hiked up the ridge back of camp and found where one wolf had sat in the snow and warily watched the intruders in his domain.

As late as 1920, the wolves were quite a menace in the valley—especially in winter when the snow got deep. They would kill numerous deer and elk rendered helpless by the deep snow. One wolf would go up on the mountain and chase the animals toward the river. The others in the wolf pack would lie in wait and intercept the fleeing animals before they reached the river. The wolves would kill for the fun of it, not eating all the kills they made. During the severe winter of 1919, two wolves were seen in the road near Nimrod, and their tracks were everywhere. The low ridges where the deer were wintering were a veritable slaughtering ground for the wolves.

Now the wolves are all gone from this area, and, in fact, no authentic sightings have been made in all Oregon. One regrets the passing of the gray wolf, as he created many hair-raising stories, and has remained a legend for many years in the West.

# ADAPTABLE COYOTE

Old man coyote sat on a high ridge and gave his hunting call.

It was early evening, and he was calling his family together for the night hunt. From far out on the desert he was answered by his mate, followed by the yapping of the young coyotes from a nearby butte.

This early evening serenade takes place nightly, and, in a few short barks and a long drawn out howl, plans are made for the evening hunt.

Coyotes weigh from twenty-five to forty pounds. They are generally gray in color, but vary a great deal, depending on the locality in which they live. Some of the mountain coyotes are almost black. At a distance they could be mistaken for a German shepherd.

Their den is in the rocks of a high ridge or may be dug in almost any well-hidden area. Two to six pups are born in the spring, and the parents both hunt to bring them food, which may include rabbits, rats, squirrels, birds and sometimes even a snake. The most readily available game is taken. When the pups are old enough to follow the parents, they are taught to hunt.

Probably no animal is so maligned and persecuted as the coyote. He is shot, trapped, poisoned, chased by dogs, and hunted from planes; yet he still thrives and learns to adapt himself to the changing conditions. He can live in the desert or mountains or make his home at the edge of a big city.

In his original environment he was a desert dweller, but the coming of man changed all of this. Now the coyote has learned to live near man, to eat new foods and to be constantly alert for new dangers.

He is blamed for many things he does not do. Chief of these is killing sheep. Perhaps a sheep has been killed by dogs, but the coyote gets the blame. A deer is found and coyote tracks are nearby. The immediate assumption is that it is the work of a coyote. But it may have been a winter kill, or shot by man, and the coyote was cleaning it up. Sometimes, of course, he is the culprit, as witnessed in the deep snow of a hard winter when the deer are starving and cannot escape.

To point out his good traits—he will establish an ecological balance in the rabbit and rodent population if left alone. The coyote was probably put here to keep the jack rabbits and small rodents in check, and, if this relationship is disturbed by man in his extermination campaigns, some kind of population explosion will result.

Many stories have been told of the amazing intelligence of the coyote, and many are probably true. Any trapper who has tried to deal with some wily old killer coyote can verify this.

# PREDATORS OF ACTION

We were watching a grey squirrel busily cutting cones from a fir tree. High in the top he wove an endless pattern, traveling from one cone-heavy branch to another. At each fleeting stop, a cone would fall. Sometimes several cones would be in the air at the same time. The noise of the squirrel's work could be heard all over the forest. Suddenly, from out of the sky, a diving hawk appeared. Without apparently checking his swift dive, he hit the squirrel and knocked him to the ground. In his return swoop, he picked up the limp body and flew away.

The endless stalk of the predator for his prey is a common sight in nature. Hawks, owls, coyotes, cougars, eagles, fish ducks and many more birds and animals all depend on the hunt and must kill for their food. Nature has arranged prolific breeding in some species. They must be controlled by predators, or their great numbers will eventually spell death for all.

A coyote can be seen hunting in the meadows. He is intently watching the grass just ahead. As he walks he seems almost to be floating over the field, scarcely disturbing the grass. Then, suddenly, he jumps into a clump of waving tops and comes up with a wriggling mouse in his mouth. A gulp, and the last thing you see is the tail going down his throat.

A kingfisher sits motionless on a dead limb a few feet over the water. In a flash, he dives head first into the river and emerges with a tiny fingerling in his bill. An osprey flies over the lake and occasionally hovers over the surface. With the same incredible speed as the hawk, he dives and hits feet first.

With a terrific splashing of water he comes up with a six-inch fish in his claws.

A mountain lion, or cougar as they are called in this area, will hunt silently through the woods, testing every breeze for the scent of game. His trail will be winding as the vagaries of the wind bring him the promise of game. A careful stalk, coupled with a terrifically fast dash, will be rewarded with a kill. Perhaps this time it is a rabbit that satisfies the cougar's hunger.

An eagle flying over the river or marsh will spot a flock of ducks. Time after time he will dive at them, only to have the ducks disappear under the water and elude him. But the ducks are getting tired, and, on one fateful dive, he rises swiftly with a duck in his powerful claws.

The many predators, armed with their various array of weapons, such as teeth, claws beaks or talons, must constantly hunt to supply their needs. And in this hunting, they are performing a duty given them by nature. They are keeping a species of fish, bird, or animal in check and are taking the sick, weak, or unwary from the species, leaving a healthy few to propagate their kind.

# MOUNTAIN HARVESTER

We were camped in a little meadow in the High Cascades. It was late summer, the valleys far below were parched by the long dry spell, but the high mountain meadow was still fresh and green. The snow had not been gone long. Scanty grass and a profusion of wild flowers reached to the base of a rock slide back of camp.

As early evening arrived, we could hear a soft, plaintive call coming from the rocks. It was difficult to locate, as though a ventriloquist were throwing his voice from place to place. To an outdoorsman, this was not a new sound, but easily identified as the lonely call of the coney (sometimes called a pika, or rock rabbit or calling hare).

These strange little animals are no larger than a squirrel, and they look like a cross between a rabbit and a rat. Their fur is brown to grey. Their small, round ears stick up like a rat's, but they have no tail. The soles of their feet are covered with fur, which gives them good traction on rocks.

Living in the rock slides, coneys make their homes under the huge boulders. Their long, sensitive whiskers and big eyes indicate that much of their life is spent in darkness. They are not completely nocturnal, but are most active in the long summer evenings. They may be heard calling any time of night.

They have two noises commonly heard. One is a loud chirp, which is a danger signal. The other is a bird-like call given several times in succession. This is the call that sounds so melancholy and lonely.

Grasses, flowers and other deciduous plants form the bulk of coney's food. In the wintertime, when everything is covered by snow, they gather and dry this vegetation on a flat rock and then pull it back into the recesses of the rock slide. They are very solicitous of their hay pile, pulling it back under a rock at the approach of a storm, and dragging it out again when the sun is shining. During the winter, when the snow is deep, they need not go out for a meal.

Hawks and owls, weasels, marten, foxes, coyotes, bobcats—all enjoy a meal from a fat coney. When danger approaches, the sentinel or watchman on a high rock gives the signal in a high-pitched "chirp." This means that the other members of the colony foraging in the meadow below must scurry for cover.

The young are born each summer and number from two to four. By early fall, they are nearly grown and ready to help in the gathering and storing of food.

By approaching a coney colony quietly, one can see them at work and perhaps be rewarded by seeing one come out from under a rock only a few feet away. Sometimes you will see a little bunch of grass moving across the meadow, followed by the tiny harvester. He seems to be pushing the grass ahead of him.

The deep snows of winter furnish the coney family with warmth and protection. They may be snowed in for six months, but far back in their homes under the rocks, they are snug and warm.

# THE BEAVER

During the hunting season this fall, I came across one of the high mountain meadows and found a little lake that had been formed by beavers damming a small stream. The pond probably covered ten acres and had a big beaver lodge at the upper end. It was a picturesque scene, with jack pines and hemlock bordering the lake, but the unusual feature about the whole thing was the dam. It was made almost entirely of rocks.

A beaver dam is ordinarily made of sticks, grass and mud, but this one had rock which almost gave it the appearance of a man-made structure. It was no doubt the work of several years—freshly placed rocks showed that it had been recently repaired. Each season the beavers would add a few stones, along with mud and sticks. In time the vegetation had decayed, leaving only the rocks held firmly together by hard mud.

Many people ask why beavers build a dam. It is for several purposes: it makes deep water and provides protection for the beavers against their enemies—the bobcat, cougar and coyote. It also floods certain areas so the beaver can readily transport materials for building his house. In a cold country, it is important to have deep water for protection against the winter. When the pond freezes over, the beaver is secure against both the predatory animals and the freezing temperatures. He will come out under the ice and go about his business of keeping the dam repaired, and will eat bark from his supply of sticks stored under the water.

The beaver prefers the inner bark of cottonwood, aspen and

willow, as well as grass and certain roots. However, he will also eat jack pine, fir, and cedar bark. The size of tree which a beaver will tackle is surprising. I have seen trees almost four feet around that a beaver has felled. Cutting through a large tree usually requires more than one season.

The beaver lodge is an interesting study both in construction and arrangement. It is a closely woven pile of sticks, grass, and mud, with several underwater entrances coming up inside the house. Above the water line will be two or three rooms, where the beavers can lie down. The lodge will have an air hole in the extreme top for ventilation. All the material composing the house will be so securely woven together that no animal can dig in. There may be from four to eight beavers living in a lodge.

Beavers have a deep velvety fur, very rich in appearance. However, it is a heavier fur than muskrat or mink and is not so much in demand for coats or jackets. In recent years, the low price of beaver pelts has resulted in the gradual increase of these interesting animals in many Oregon streams.

# THE WEASEL

Suddenly you see a flash of movement on a snow background. You look a second time, thinking that your eyes are deceiving you. It is a white weasel, with a black tip on his tail.

In the summer that same weasel turns a light brown, but with the coming of winter his coat gets snow-white. The tip of his tail and sharp little nose remain black. Thus, Mother Nature has camouflaged him for his role as a hunter.

The weasel is one of the most savage and bloodthirsty of all the predatory animals. Although he is small, weighing not more than six or eight ounces, he will catch and kill an animal ten times his size. His regular prey are mice, rats, birds, squirrels, and occasionally a rabbit. He is not adverse to raiding the chicken house, as many farmers know.

If you encounter a weasel's tracks in the snow you will see only two tiny footprints about twelve inches apart. His hind feet are placed precisely in the tracks vacated by his front feet. Some of his larger cousins, such as the mink, marten and fisher, travel the same way.

The range of the weasel is very widely distributed. One may find him almost anywhere from seashore to high mountains, but his preference is the snow country, either timbered or desert. Sometimes he may be the companion of some lonely trapper. In the high mountains, where animal life is scarce, the weasel may come around a trapping cabin and, being fed by the trapper, will in turn keep the cabin free from mice.

# PLAYFUL RIVER OTTER

A sleek brown head broke the surface of the water near the boat. With a calm deliberation that denoted a lack of fear, he scrutinized the scene carefully; then, without a ripple or splash, he disappeared below the surface of the stream. As he silently dived, his long fur tail came out of the stream. This established his identity. He was the river otter.

As distinguished from the sea otter, the river otter is found in many of our lakes and streams. He belongs to the weasel family, and, in the water, looks not much larger than a big mink. Out of the water his true size is amazing. He will weigh from twenty to thirty pounds, and his slender sinuous body will be from forty-eight to sixty inches long. Part of this length, of course, is his long tapering tail, which is fully furred. This is in contrast to the bare, scaly tail of the beaver or muskrat.

The otter is a great swimmer. He is so fast under the water that he can catch any fish. Approaching from behind, he will grab a fish in his sharp teeth, then surface to eat it leisurely on some rock or bank. It has been alleged that the otter takes a great many sporting fish, but personal observations indicate that he takes the fish most readily available, often trash fish such as suckers or squaw fish.

A favorite food is crayfish. I have often seen an otter dive to the bottom of a lake and come up with a crayfish in his mouth. The noise of his cracking and eating can be heard several hundred feet away.

The otter is playful. An entire otter family will play a game of hide and seek in the water. It will begin as follow the leader. As the individuals dive and swim under the water, they will occasionally surface and utter a shrill chirp or whistle as if to say, "Here I am!" Sometimes they will use their otter slides for play. An otter slide is a steep bank of mud above a pool which they keep slick and wet by repeatedly climbing out of the water and sliding down the incline into the pool. Life is all play for the young otters. When they are out on a sand bank, they frolic like kittens.

The young, numbering from two to four, are born in the spring. The den will be under a log drift or deep in a hole among the rocks. A fine gray underfur, topped with longer brown outer fur, keeps the young warm and dry. The fur is in great demand by the fur trade and is one of the most durable of all animal furs.

Young otters make fine pets. They are easily housebroken and can be taught to follow like a dog. Not unlike seals, they have a high degree of intelligence and can be trained as retrievers in the water.

On one of the famous river trips in Oregon—from Grants Pass to Gold Beach on the Rogue River—one may see a great many otters. Sometimes it will be a lone otter running along the bank, but more often it will be whole families sunning on the rocks or fishing in a riffle. They are curious animals and seem to pose for pictures obligingly.

# A BUSY COLLECTOR

We were camped at an old cabin on the Rogue River. Dark clouds were scudding across the sky, so we prepared to sleep in the shelter. Beds were spread on the floor, and, as the first hard patter of raindrops hit, we turned in for the night.

It was morning before we realized that we had a nocturnal visitor. When one of my companions started to lace his boots, he noticed that the laces were cut and parts of them missing. About the same time, my other companion was searching for his gloves. Our night visitor was a wood rat. After considerable search, we discovered the pack rat's snug nest under the floor of the cabin. Laying right on top of all the debris were the gloves.

The wood rat, sometimes known as the pack rat or cave rat, is found throughout Oregon. His nests are found in wooded areas, around rimrocks or rock slides, or even in the deserts of Eastern Oregon.

He uses any available material that will make a mound. It may be sticks, cones, rocks, cowchips or any material discarded by man. The pile may cover several square feet and resembles a beaver house. In the forest the nest will sometimes be constructed of the branches of small trees and will be surrounded by a clear area in which all the smaller trees have been killed.

The nest is usually occupied by only one rat, except at mating time or during the rearing of the young. As each young rat reaches maturity, he leaves home and builds his own nest.

A wood rat's nest is similar to the collection of some frugal person's accumulation of many years. Bits of paper, string, an old shoe, tin cans, pine cones, and unusual rocks all add to the pile. An irritated husband might compare his thrifty wife's tendencies to those of a pack rat.

The huge pile of material in the nest is for warmth and protection. By the time a predator, such as a bobcat, coyote or skunk, has dug through the pile, the rat has made his escape. Under the heap will be a series of runways, with rooms for food storage and a soft nest for sleeping.

The Oregon woodrat is not to be confused with the ordinary wharf rat, which has a slick tail. The wood rat of the far west has a furred tail, long whiskers for nocturnal prowling, bright intelligent eyes, and white feet. He has well-furred ears and a soft fluffy coat. He has a very distinctive odor, which you may have noticed around an abandoned cabin. With the coming of fall, there is always a migration of rats from the woods to buildings, where shelter is sought for the winter.

The name "trade rat" is also given to the wood rat. He sometimes has the habit of taking some object and leaving another in its place. He loves to pick up bright or unusual objects. A wristwatch left around camp may disappear. A knife, fork, or spoon is a favorite prize. I even recall an incident where a rat stole a man's false teeth. They were found the next morning on top of the rat's nest.

Wood rats have the habit of thumping their feet on the ground when alarmed or annoyed, but for the most part they are friendly fellows and might be called the little clowns of the woods.

# OREGON NEWCOMER

A fat, waddling porcupine was coming down the trail. As he ambled along, singing his little chuckling song, he was completely at peace with the world. His only thought was another good tree to climb, where he would spend several days feeding on the swelling buds and juicy bark. But this would not come to pass. A sinister stranger was on his trail, and soon one of nature's wild dramas would be enacted.

The stranger was a fisher, arch enemy of the porcupine. As he swiftly approached the porcupine, the quilly pig sensed the danger and quickly rolled himself into a ball, with sharp quills sticking out in all directions. With extreme caution, the fisher circled the porcupine several times, then darted in and deftly rolled him over with a quick flip of a paw. The vulnerable underside of the porcupine was now exposed, and a quick kill was made.

Fishers were recently re-introduced to Oregon. They were live-trapped in British Columbia by Canadian trappers and released in several wild areas.

A fisher is one of the larger members of the weasel family. His close cousins are the mink and marten. He is a dark brown to black animal, rather slender, weighing from four to twelve pounds. He is equally at home in the trees or on the ground. His habit of hunting alone and covering many miles of forest trails makes him a solitary and unsociable wanderer.

In his travels, which are mostly at night, he spends a great deal of his time in the trees, where he can readily catch squirrels, birds or sometimes his smaller cousin, the marten. On the ground he will hunt rabbits, grouse, mice or any other small game. Being a fierce fighter, he needs only to fear man or other large predators.

His den may be a hole in a tree, a hollow log or even a cavity in a rock cliff. Two or three young make up a litter; after several months they are old enough to accompany their mother on hunts. As soon as they learn to hunt well, they disband and go their lonely ways.

In the early days of the fur trade, many fishers were trapped in Oregon, but because of the great demand for their fur, they were soon trapped out. They were re-introduced to the woods in hope that they would help control the porcupine population.

At the present time, their furs are the most valuable of all wild fur-bearing animals. Most of the fishers come from Canada, where trapping them is still allowed. Since they are nocturnal animals of the deep forests, one would be fortunate to see fishers in their natural habitat.

# THE BLACK BEAR

Just about this time of year, the black bear has eaten his last meal of mushrooms and is looking for a place to sleep the winter through. For the past month he has been eating continuously. Unlike some people, the bear is trying to put on fat. He needs this stored-up energy for the long winter months of hibernation.

During the spring and early summer months, when bears first emerge from their long sleep, they feed on grass and young green plants. From time to time their diet may be supplemented with the meat of the winter-killed elk or deer. Later on, when the first berries ripen, they will change their diet again. Late summer brings many different kinds of berries. The salal berry is a favorite with bears, as is the mountain blueberry or huckleberry. Before these ripen, the manzanita berry has been a big item on his menu.

Along with his diet of plants and berries, the black bear is not adverse to robbing a camp for anything that is edible. One fall we were elk hunting, and everybody had left camp early in the morning to hunt all day. Sometime during the day a bear invaded camp and sampled all the food we had. He bit into every can and crushed it, if it tasted good. The only things he did not like were pickles and spaghetti.

In their eating habits, the bears are almost completely omnivorous. They will dig out an ant's nest and lick up the ants, or rob a bee tree whenever they are fortunate enough to find one. Their heavy coat protects them from the stings of the angry bees. Sometimes bears will strip a young fir tree to get the sap and inner bark, and they are known to come into orchards and damage fruit trees occasionally.

I have even known bears to eat each other. Two different falls we have killed bears while elk hunting and have hung the carcasses in a tree to pick up later. Other bears have found them and completely cleaned them up.

The last food bears seek in the fall is mushrooms. These are found in great abundance in the high meadows after the first fall rains. The early snow storms may cover the mushrooms, but a bear will find them under several inches of snow and root them out like a hog.

During this search for food, the bear is also on the lookout for a good den for the winter. This may be a hollow tree or log, a dry cave, or even a big pile of brush that the bear gets together. He will use this den for awhile, coming out at infrequent intervals to feed. Then some cold snowy morning, he will sleep in for his long winter hibernation.

# BEARS LEAVING SNUG DENS

With the coming of the first warm days of spring, the black bears will arouse from their long winter's sleep. For four or five months, they have been in the deep sleep of hibernation. In a dry cave, under a big windfall or in a hollow tree, they have made their den and perhaps gathered dry leaves or other material to make it a snug place. No winter storm disturbed them, and deep snow only made their den a more secure home. Now, as the weather grows warmer, they awake and start the never-ending search for food. They are as "hungry as bears."

The first food they find will probably be the new tender grass on an open hillside, or it may be a winterkill of some deer or elk. A bear will eat practically anything. With the coming of early summer, a few berries will appear, and, by mid-summer, food is abundant everywhere. In areas where food is not available, the black bears will peel a Douglas fir tree and eat the sweet inner cambium layer. The foresters and tree farmers are not their friends.

An average-sized black bear will weigh from 150 to 250 pounds. Although he is normally black, his color will vary from jet black to a light brown. A black mother may have brown cubs and vice versa. The young, usually two, are born during the late months of winter while the mother is still in hibernation. For some time they live off their mother's milk, even though she does not have food. Her surplus fat furnishes the necessary nourishment. When the young are first born, they are the smallest of any animal in comparison to the adult. The mother may weigh 200 pounds and the babies only a few ounces.

By the time the hibernating bears are ready to come out of their dens, the cubs are well developed and ready to follow their mother. Now comes the never ending search for food.

Last summer, while we were camped at Erma Bell Lakes, an old bear and her young started coming into the camping area and feeding in the open garbage pits. Word got out that ferocious bears were terrorizing people around camp, and soon a big brave hunter, armed with a high-powered rifle, appeared.

He shot the mother bear and wounded her in a front leg. Several times, just at dusk or daylight, we saw the old mother limping through the woods, followed by the little cubs. Now she could no longer forage food for them, so they started coming boldly into camp and raiding the cook tent. One early morning we captured one of the little cubs and tied him to a tree with a rope and collar. We kept him for a few hours for pictures and then turned him loose. Away he ran up into the woods and never returned. His frightening experience was too much.

A black bear is the clown of the wilderness. He will slide down a snowbank like a child on a sled or climb a tree and play for hours. It is extremely interesting to watch a bear in his natural environment. But many hunters cannot resist shooting every bear they see, even though they do not use them. Bears should be protected by law; they seldom do real damage.

Now it is fall again, and the bears are eating great amounts to accumulate fat for the long winter months to come. Berries are everywhere, and the big tasty mushrooms are beginning to show on the ridges. In their wanderings, bears are probably on the lookout for a good den. As the days grow shorter and the first big fall storms come, they begin to disappear.

It is back to their dens for another long winter's sleep.

# WINTERING GROUNDS

This is the domain of the deer and elk. High in the Cascades, the South Fork valley extends almost to the summer snow line. Great mountains rise on either side. It is wild country, far from civilization, and well suited for the large herds of elk and deer that annually come here to winter.

A wintering ground must have several features: open south slopes where the snow melts early, brush hillsides where the animals can feed, and a labyrinth of deer and elk trails that can be kept open during winters of deep snow. This last feature is extremely important, for in times of heavy snowfall the animals travel in all directions, feeding as they go, breaking new paths. In this manner they can reach the browse and also have room to run if predatory animals attack.

A well-traveled wintering ground is called a "yarding ground." Here the animals congregate and wait out a heavy storm. Sometimes the browse on smaller bushes gets so scarce that the large animals must "walk down" larger trees. A big elk will straddle a willow, maple or madronna and bend it over, eating the small shoots and leaves. At times like this, the smaller animals, such as deer, will follow an elk and enjoy the meal with him. Several times I have noted small deer following an elk and nibbling off the tip of a tree that the larger animal is holding down.

This is the time of year when elk congregate in large herds. Herding is probably an age-old instinct for the protection of the young; older animals will form a circle, keeping the calves in the center, when predatory animals threaten the herd. Another protection for the grazing animals is the presence of lakes or streams. A closely pursued animal will go straight for water and seek safety by swimming or standing in water where coyotes or wolves will not go.

Even in summer, the wintering grounds can be recognized by the maize of well-traveled trails, heavily browsed brush, shed antlers, and an occasional pile of bones where either winter or a predatory animal has taken its toll. It is in the winter that most of the wild animals die.

In the deep snow, the deer and elk are more vulnerable to cougars, wolves and coyotes. Crusted snow is deadly then because the smaller hooves of the deer will break through, while the coyote can run along on top and easily make his kill. The elk do not fear the coyote, but a cougar or pack of wolves will wreak havoc with an elk herd. All the gray wolves are gone from this country, but there still remain a few cougars.

With the coming of spring and the melting snow, the elk and deer will slowly work back into the higher country, to the meadows and high ridges where they will spend the summer.

# ANTLERS SHED YEARLY

A few days ago I had the rare experience of seeing a buck shed one of his horns. We were floating down the river when we saw a magnificent buck standing by the water's edge.

On our approach, he bounded away in great leaps and disappeared into a dense thicket of firs. Just as he made the first jump, one of his horns hit a vine maple and was knocked completely off. He vanished, a one-sided buck. Later on we picked up the horn and noted how it had torn from his head, with barely a blood spot to show where it had been.

It is an accepted fact that each year most deer and elk shed their horns. They may be the short, sharp spikes of a yearling animal or the tremendous six-foot spread of a bull elk.

The complete set of horns, no matter how large, is dropped during the winter months and another one grown for the next season. The growth must be accomplished in a comparatively short time, the velvet rubbed off clean, and the horns sharpened and tested for the rutting season in the fall.

By the time a male deer or elk is a yearling, he will start to grow horns. In the first year he will show short spikes. Each succeeding year, until an animal reaches full maturity, the horn growth will be greater and have more points. But the number of points does not necessarily indicate the age of the animal. It is only an approximation.

After reaching the prime of life, the animal's horns start

getting more rugged. More points will occur with many little nodules and some roughness. An old animal may support a freak set of horns.

# FRIENDLY BLACKTAIL

The doe came down the trail so quietly that we were first aware of her when she was standing about a hundred feet away.

She remained motionless under a fir tree, but, as we made no sudden movements, she approached our fire. We continued conversing quietly, and the soft music of guitar and harmonica went on, but these things did not alarm her. She circled the fire cautiously and found the stump where we had been pouring the extra bacon fat. Here she stopped and began licking hungrily.

Deer are smart enough to know that where humans are there will be salt. There are places in the mountains where there are natural salt licks, and these are regularly frequented by both deer and elk.

The next evening the doe was followed by a buck with long slender spikes in velvet, and a few days later she brought her fawns down. She was very nervous when she had them with her, and we could hear her snorting and giving them warning. This snort is made by the sudden expulsion of air through the nostrils and has a whistling sound which carries quite a distance through the woods.

Deer have their fawns in late May and early June. Twin fawns, one a buck and one a doe, are the usual rule. When fawns are first born they have no scent, and the mother hides them in the brush while she goes away to feed. This lack of scent, coupled with their spotted protective coloring, is their prime protection against predators. Many predators in Oregon have been killed off, so in some cases man has become the only balancing agent for deer.

There are two kinds of deer in Oregon—the black tail in Western Oregon and the mule deer in eastern areas of the state. A smaller black tail is found on the coast, and occasionally a white tail is found.

Mule deer have had a tendency in the last few years to come over the summit of the Cascades and mingle with the black tail in the Three Sisters region. Black tail, however, do not generally travel into Eastern Oregon.

Deer are quite friendly to humans, and we have had many experiences in the woods to demonstrate this. On one occasion we were camped out with a family from New York. We slept in the open, as the mosquito season was past, and had made our beds in a high mountain meadow.

In the middle of the night we heard a small girl call out, "Mommy, come quick! This deer is looking at me."

Only a few feet away a deer stood almost over the child's sleeping bag, as if curiously investigating the strange object she had found in her feeding grounds. As flashlights began showing, she bound away. Later, this same doe came back to camp often and lost her fear to the extent of taking bread from the small girl's hand.

# COUGAR STORY

Many hair-raising stories have been told about the cougar. Some are just good campfire stories, while others are true.

This story happens to be in the latter category. One fall, many years ago, an old-timer living at McKenzie Bridge was hired to guide a "city feller" on a deer hunting trip. They packed their equipment on their backs and set off up the mountain to an old hunting camp used by the guide.

Late that evening, as they approached the camp, the dude swore he saw something leave the shelter, which was back under an overhanging bank. A closer examination showed that something or someone had been lying on a bed of boughs. The dude was even sure that the bed was still warm.

Nevertheless, they camped there. The old-timer was completely unperturbed about the whole thing, thinking that probably his companion, being unused to the wilderness, was using his imagination.

That evening, as they were retiring for the night, the dude suggested that one of them should keep watch while the other slept. He would keep the first watch and wake his guide at a designated time. The guide agreed to this and immediately turned in. In the back of his mind was this plan—when it came his turn to watch, he would wait until the hunter went to sleep, then crawl back into bed himself.

At the appointed hour, the nervous sentinel woke his

companion to take the second watch. He reported that something had been walking back and forth just out of the firelight. The guide reassured him and told him to get some sleep.

It was late, and the fire had burned down to a bed of coals. The old-timer was leaning back against the base of a tree and almost dozing off. Suddenly, he was aware of two green eyes across the dying fire. With great care he slowly raised his rifle and fired. A tremendous thrashing in the brush brought the hunter out of his sleeping bag and ready to run. But the shot had found its mark, and there lay a big female cougar.

What made the cougar want this particular bed always remained a mystery. But from that time on, the old-timer listened with great respect to his dudes' cougar stories.

# THE COUGAR'S SCREAM

If you want to start a good argument among outdoorsmen just ask the question, "Does a cougar scream?" The answer that most conservative hunters will make is that they have never heard one.

I have personally contacted several experienced cougar hunters, and their answers have been the same. They acknowledge that a cougar will growl or snarl when treed by dogs, but that they personally have never heard one make any other noise.

Many noises heard in the woods could be interpreted as the scream of a cougar, such as two trees rubbing together when the wind is blowing, the last notes of a long drawn-out coyote howl or the blood-curdling screech of an owl.

Many years ago, when I was working in the Forest Service, another boy and I were clearing a trail in the Indian Ridge area. We were following a dim path through the very heavy timber, when all of a sudden there rose the most unearthly sound a man ever heard. It was coming from a little thicket several hundred feet ahead. The noise at times was like a scream, then dying away into a terrible moan. It rose and fell as the wind sighed through the trees.

We were not especially scared, as we had good sharp axes, so we decided to separate, each circling the thicket on opposite sides. As we got closer, the noise seemed to be coming from high in the trees. It proved to be two small firs rubbing together in the gentle wind. Several times later, I was past that spot and heard the same noise.            .

Another time we were camped in the Separation Valley. We had killed an elk that day and packed it into camp where the bears couldn't get it. Several times that night we heard a high-pitched wail that sounded unlike any of the usual noises of the woods. Finally we decided it was a young coyote that was omitting the short staccato barks from of his call, and all we were hearing was the last long howl. Next morning the tracks in the snow proved us right.

But it would detract from the mystery and excitement of the woods to know that a cougar doesn't scream. Let's string along with the myth in hopes that some day we may get to hear one.

# BEAR CLAW CABIN

In a hidden ravine in Mink Lake Basin stands an old trapper's cabin, the scene of a battle between a big bear and a man.

Many years ago when marten, fox and ermine were selling at a good price, an old trapper ran a trap line through this high country. Each fall he would outfit the cabins and, when trapping season opened, would set a line of traps. The trap line was some 60 miles long with cabins located a day's hike apart. This was trapping in the deep snow and using either snow-shoes or skis, as the snow conditions demanded.

On this particular day a big snow storm had hit and going was very tough. The trapper knew he would be late reaching the cabin near Mink Lake, but he must push on as the weather was too severe to spend the night out.

As he approached the cabin about 8 o'clock that night, he had the feeling that something was wrong. Out of the gloom and thick falling snow a huge black bear appeared. With a loud surprised "woof", it whirled and ran for a nearby thicket. A quick glance showed that the bear had been trying to break into the cabin. The winter's provision of bacon, jerky and other food had attracted him.

Although the cabin was sturdily constructed of logs, with shakes on the roof, he had literally torn it to pieces. One whole side of the shake roof was torn off. The stove pipe was crushed and the only window broken. Several inches of new fallen snow covered the inside of the cabin. In order to survive, the trapper must patch the roof, repair the stove pipe, shovel the snow out and get a fire going.

Very slowly and with numbed hands, he dug the torn shakes from under the snow and nailed them back on the roof. His only light to work by was a "pilooser," a candle stuck in a tin can. The stove pipe had to be straightened and put in place. It was nearly midnight when he made a batch of biscuits and cooked a hot meal.

As the fire died down and everything was quiet, the trapper heard a faint sniffing at the door. Very quietly he grabbed his loaded gun and slipped to the door, opened it a tiny crack and peeked out. The bear was standing not 20 feet away but instantly whirled and ran for the timber.

Although the bear presented a good silhouette against the background of snow, it was, nevertheless, a difficult shot. The trapper was sure he had scored a hit, but decided to wait until morning before investigating.

Even before daylight he was awake and preparing for a long chase. In any event, whether the bear was wounded or not, he was determined to track him down and kill him. The bear had already done a great deal of damage to the cabin and would return if left alone.

As the first gray daylight appeared, the trapper closed the cabin door and walked across the opening into the trees where the bear was last seen. There were his tracks in the soft snow and 50 feet further on were signs of blood. A light snow had sifted through the trees during the later part of the night, but the tracks were easy to follow. Under the thick trees the snow was not deep, but out in the openings the bear was plunging through deep soft drifts. When he would brush by a tree or bank of snow, the telltale blood indicated he was hit high in the left side.

His general direction of flight was downhill, and probably a half mile from the cabin he had stopped in a hemlock thicket and laid down. During the early morning hours he had moved around, bedding down several times. Each bed showed he was bleeding badly. A little farther on the tracks were very fresh. The bear jumped and ran as the trapper entered the far side of the thicket.

Then began a race of endurance. The huge bear was sinking deeply in the soft snow, but the trapper was using snowshoes. At times the trapper was so close on the trail that bits of snow would be rolling back into the bear's tracks. Coming up on a little ridge he got a glimpse of the bear disappearing over the next rise. A few minutes later he saw the bear again, and this time he got in another shot.

A fresh spray of blood on the snow indicated another hit. The bear couldn't possibly last much longer. His tracks now led into a dense hemlock thicket, and just as the trapper's eyes got accustomed to the gloom, a huge black shape rose suddenly not 40 feet away. With a terrible snarl of rage the bear charged, but two more fast shots dropped him in his tracks.

The chase was over, but the trapper was many miles from his cabin and darkness was not far away. He must spend the night there, so he cut down a dead tree and started a fire. Skinning the bear took a couple of hours, but when he had finished he also had his bed for the night. Laying the big fur on the snow (skin side down), he slept on half of the rug and folded the other half over him. Curled up in the bear's skin he slept the deep sleep of exhaustion.

The trapper's cabin still stands in the Mink Lake Basin not far from the Skyline Trail. The claw and tooth marks on the logs are evidence of this long ago battle.

# SHORTY AND THE BEAR

Way back in the summer of 1927, I was working on a trail crew in the Forest Service, and we were packing back on the Olallie trail. Our job was to clear the trail of all fallen trees from the previous winter and repair the telephone lines.

We had spent several days on the trail from McKenzie Bridge to Bear Flat and had camped that evening at the edge of a little meadow. The horses were hobbled and turned out to feed, and we made our night's camp under some big trees. Packs were laying all around on the ground, and each man selected his place to spread his blankets. We didn't have sleeping bags in those days.

Along in the middle of the night I was awakened by some unusual noise. The moonlight was filtering down through the trees, and each man could be seen rolled up tightly in his blanket.

Suddenly, out of the shadows, appeared a little bear. He couldn't have been bigger than a cocker spaniel. He sniffed around the camp a little, picking up a morsel of food here and there; then he walked by the packer's bed. The packer was a small bald-headed man called "Shorty," and, as he lay sleeping, his very bald head was quite obvious sticking out of his blanket roll.

The little bear walked up to Shorty and actually licked his bald head.

Shorty later said the bear's tongue felt like sandpaper. With a start he awakened and saw the bear standing there. He gave one awful yell and lit a-running. This, of course, aroused the camp.

When the flashlights were turned on there sat Shorty, not three feet from the ground, but hugging a big fir tree for dear life. Later he said he was positive that he was up in that tree 30 or 40 feet! That tree saved a man's life, and we hope the loggers never cut it.

# FAMOUS COUGAR HUNTER

One of the most famous cougar hunters Oregon has known lived at McKenzie Bridge and spent most of his time in the woods trapping or hunting for the big predatory cats. His record of 44 cougars in four years probably still stands as tops.

The following story was told to me by the well-known hunter and substantiates a few facts we have heard about cougars. In the late fall he was on one of his long trips in the woods. Together with his old cougar dog, Fritz, he was camped at the old Dompier cabin on the South Fork of the McKenzie. A storm during the night had deposited six inches of fresh snow. As he stepped out of the cabin the next morning to get a pail of water from the stream, he noticed that the snow had been freshly disturbed on a small log spanning the river. A closer examination showed that a big cougar had crossed during the night and headed for the open hillside on the east side of the river. This country was the wintering ground of numerous deer and elk.

A half hour after the discovery, the hunter and his equally well-known cougar hound were on the trail. The tracks led up the steep slope out of the canyon. From his seemingly erratic course, the hunter knew the big cat was testing the wind in search of game to kill.

A half mile further on, the stalk had been completed and the big cougar had killed a full grown cow elk. Signs indicated that the elk had been dragged several hundred feet down into a thicket; then apparently before the cougar could eat his fill, two black bears had arrived on the scene and driven the killer away.

All this time the dog was anxious to go, but it was the hunter's method of hunting to jump the cougar first, then turn the dog loose.

A half mile further on, the cougar had made another kill. This time it was a forked-horn buck. He had been partly eaten, and, from the actions of the dog, the hunter knew the cougar was on the run with the dog close behind. After a short chase, the barking changed to the sharp staccato baying which meant that the quarry had been treed.

This was the exciting climax and the reward for a grueling chase for both the dog and man. As the hunter approached the tree, he could see the big tawny cat crouched upon a limb 30 feet up. With a-well aimed shot from his 30 Lugar pistol, another chase was ended. This cougar was one of the largest he had ever killed, weighing as much as a large man. No wonder the elk and deer herds suffer when a killer like this is stalking their trails.

# MURDER AT LAVA LAKE

This is the story that none but the old-timers remember, a true story of an unsolved murder in the High Cascades.

Back in about 1919, three boys from Bend decided to spend a winter trapping in high mountains. They were inexperienced but decided that there was safety in numbers and that three could meet any emergencies. In the late fall they packed back into the mountains and built a cabin at Little Lava Lake, the extreme headwaters of the Deschutes River.

Supplies for the winter were packed in, enough wood to last was cut and traplines laid out. Along with the necessary supplies, they decided to take in two pairs of very valuable silver foxes. The thought was that the cold climate would produce an exceptionally fine fur on the foxes and that, when they were prime, they would be pelted. At that time silver foxes were quite rare and commanded a very high price.

When the boys left home they reassured their parents that they would be safe and that if they didn't come out at Christmas time, not to worry. Snow conditions might be unfavorable for traveling or the trapping might keep them on the lines.

The holiday season passed and the boys didn't come out, but their folks were not concerned as all three boys were together. Then the end of trapping season arrived and still the boys didn't come home. By that time a search party was organized.

When the search party reached Little Lava Lake, they found

nothing but a mound of snow where the cabin had stood. Four feet of snow covered the burned cabin. The fox pens were empty and there was no sign of the boys. A search of the area disclosed a hole cut in the ice of the lake and the bodies of the boys crammed through the hole. Two of the boys had been shot, and the third had been killed with an axe. The depth of the snow over the burned cabin indicated that the murder had been committed about Christmas time.

The icy winter had covered all possible clues. The fox skins were found in a warehouse in Portland, but the owner got wind that the skins were being watched and never came back.

This was the beginning of the myth that a madman was running loose in the Cascades. Many incidents in the following years lent credence to this story. In a later article I will tell you some of the stories.

# WILDMAN OF THE CASCADES

In the years after the triple murder at Lava Lake, there were some strange events. Campers reported prowlers around their camps at night. Hunters and trappers in that region told of a mysterious visitor who would come at night, make weird noises to scare them, and leave big footprints in the dust or snow. These stories led to the supposition that there was a mad man living in the High Cascades.

One fall two trappers packed their provisions into the Horse Lake area and built cabins in preparation for winter trapping. The cabins were about six miles apart. Each man would live in his own cabin but check in with his partner every so often for company and trapping news. When the first snows of the winter came, it found the trappers busy taking fur.

One morning one of the trappers rose early and stepped outside to note the new snowfall. The first thing he saw was the fresh track of a big man who, during the night, had walked up to his window. This immediately recalled stories of the madman so, without even eating breakfast, he grabbed his gun and set out for his partner's cabin.

About halfway there he met his partner who reported the same strange behavior of a nocturnal visitor. This was too much for the trappers. They immediately started for civilization.

The next fall a group of deer hunters had packed into Horse Lake and made camp in the old cabin. During the day, while they were away, someone pinned the coffee pot to the door with a big knife. That night someone prowled around the cabin and kept the dog barking all night. Although the hunters were seasoned woodsmen, these events were beginning to get on their nerves. That night a shot rang out. The next day they noticed tracks just outside the cabin. This was too much, even for brave men. They packed up and hit the trail.

Another story deals with a Forest Service man who camped at Scott Lake. He had just arrived for the summer and had camped outside the shelter, making his bed within a few feet of the campfire. During the night a big man had walked up to his bed, leaving his tracks in the dust between the bed and the campfire. This experience didn't run the Forest Service man out of the mountains, but thereafter he carried a gun strapped on his hip.

These stories were told for many years, but were gradually forgotten. Some people finally concluded that a trapper had probably committed the murder at Lava Lake and subsequent acts, as a means of scaring intruders out of his territory.